*I am overwhelmed and brought to tears by reading this book. I feel as if Pearl is present with me now.*

-Julie S. G., New York

*This is destined to be a classic—a must-read for every sincere seeker.*

-Daye P., Laguna Beach, California

*The moment I picked up Peter's insightful book on Pearl, I felt her warm presence and knew she had deep wisdom to share with me.*

-Violet S., Mount Shasta, California

*I cherish every moment I spent with Pearl. It is as though [those moments] were outside of what we call time.*

-Michael T., Clearlake, California

*I could not put the book down, there was such a thrill of excitement. I could feel the ripple effect of Peter's meeting with Pearl in my heart.*

-Christine O., Redwood City, California

# *Lady Master Pearl*

## *My Teacher*

### *By*
### *Peter Mt. Shasta*

Church of the Seven Rays
P. O. Box 1103
Mount Shasta, California 96067
U.S.A.

Copyright 2015 Peter Mt. Shasta. All rights reserved.

ISBN 978-0-9984143-0-0

Published by Church of the Seven Rays
Previously published as an eBook by Smashwords.com

By the same author:

***"I AM" the Open Door***
(M. S. Princess, 1978)

***"I AM" Affirmations
and the Secret of their Effective Use***
(Church of the Seven Rays, 2012)

***Adventures of a Western Mystic, Part I:
Search for the Guru***
(Church of the Seven Rays, 2014)

***Adventures of a Western Mystic, Part II:
Apprentice to the Masters***
(Church of the Seven Rays, 2010)

Website and blog: www.PeterMtShasta.com

Cover by Messuti Productions

## *Dedication*

*This book is dedicated to the students of Pearl,
past, present and future.*

# Contents

Acknowledgements ............................................................. 9
Foreword ............................................................................ 11
Esotericism in the West.................................................... 15
Saint Germain .................................................................... 19
The I AM Presence ........................................................... 21
Preface ................................................................................ 23

1. Mountain Girl ................................................................ 27
2. A Mysterious Woman Appears .................................. 31
3. First Job, First Man ...................................................... 35
4. Good Deed .................................................................... 39
5. Saint Germain Appears ................................................ 41
6. Experiencing an Ascended Master ............................ 45
7. Saving a City and Bridge ............................................. 49
8. A Master's Request ...................................................... 53
9. Incurring the Wrath of Beloved Mama ..................... 57
10. Meeting of the Twin Rays ......................................... 61
11. A Lady Master to the Rescue .................................... 65
12. Pearl Stirs Up a Firestorm ......................................... 69
13. The Ascension of Godfre Ray King ......................... 73
14. Who is the Next Messenger? .................................... 77
15. Romance, Marriage, and Divorce ............................. 87
16. Pearl and the United Nations ................................... 95
17. Lady Master Leto's Reprimand ............................... 101
18. UFO Visitors .............................................................. 105
19. Mount Shasta Calls .................................................... 109
20. Haight-Ashbury .......................................................... 113
21. Two Sent by the Masters .......................................... 117

22. I Meet Pearl .................................................... 121
23. We Invoke Saint Germain ............................... 127
24. The Magic Switchboard ................................. 137
25. Challenges ...................................................... 141
26. A Near Ascension .......................................... 149
27. Pearl's Advice to Women ............................... 153
28. You Are Ready ............................................... 157
29. An Inner Marriage .......................................... 163
30. Pearl and Jerry ................................................ 165
31. Step By Step We Climb ................................. 169
32. Bill's Revelation ............................................. 179
33. Pearl's Ascension ........................................... 181

Postscript: A Note on Historical Accuracy .................... 185

Read Other Books by Peter Mt. Shasta .......................... 187

## *Acknowledgements*

I would like to thank Steve Bollock, Karen Carty, Carl Marsak, Gabriel Messuti, Pete and Patti Peters, Daye Proffit, Aaron Rose, and Scott Sanford for their invaluable assistance and support in the publishing of this book.

*Lady Master Pearl*

## *Foreword*

*Lady Master Pearl* is no mere chronicle of events, but a guidebook into the Light. Peter Mt. Shasta has turned his autobiographical talents to this profound biography of his beloved friend and teacher, Pearl Dorris. You will find love in its many manifestations, and deep truth within these pages that points the way clearly forward. The example of Pearl's life will change you and open up your own pathway to the Light, if you will allow it. This is a book of love and possibility, and even perhaps of inevitability.

Like Pearl Dorris herself, this small book is a quiet but mighty presence in the spiritual landscape of our Earth. Her story speaks clearly and eloquently to the times. It is a vital link in the lineage and continuity of the stewards of this knowledge of the I AM Presence. It also brings clarification and resolution to many questions and issues that have gathered around the mechanisms of delivery of this knowledge of and from the Ascended Masters. The clear message is always to seek guidance first and foremost from one's own, inner I AM Presence and develop a personal relationship with the Masters; we needn't seek permission from any other than our inner guidance.

This is an account of a natural life well lived. In this physical realm, it seems no one is immune from the tendencies and temptations of human life. Yet here we see the demonstration of evolutionary intent with its ultimate victory that holds such great hope and promise for us all. This is a book of energizing inspiration to all who seek to serve the Light. By Pearl's example, we are called to live in

Love now. Words attributed to Master Jesus come to mind, *Love one another. As I have loved you, so you must love one another. By this, everyone will know you are my disciples.*

Pearl's life was one of service and redemption, as ours can be as well. It was an opportunity for realization, which she seized. Now is the time to forge new pathways through which Illuminated Love can issue forth into every dark cranny of this blessed planet. This is the time to accept the privilege of personal responsibility. Only then can we collectively change the world.

All of us, incarnate humans and Ascended Masters alike, are made of the same stuff and are playing our vital roles in a flowing continuum of experience. One may be tempted to tarry in the eddies of the past, but the clarion call is inescapable: Now is the time to release ourselves into the full stream of glory. Now is all that I AM. Mastery is at hand for all who seek it and apply themselves to it. This is living knowledge—truly the Wisdom of the Ages—meant to be lived in the flow of life, not to stagnate in religiosity.

Pearl's story and her legacy are here carried on by Peter Mt. Shasta and surely by others of her students who continue to live their Light. What is your story? How are you contributing your unique ray in the Light? We are not here to muddle through earthly existence only to escape to some fantastic ascension beyond. We are here to infuse that heavenly realm into the experiential fabric of this sacred planet, right here, right now.

Peter Mt. Shasta's persistent message has been, in words by one known as William Shakespeare, whom many say was Saint Germain's previous incarnation:

*This above all: to thine own self be true,*
*And it must follow, as the night the day,*
*Thou canst not then be false to any man.*

For the structural integrity of any edifice, every supporting component must be strong in its individual integrity. Let this historical foundation that Peter Mt. Shasta has so lovingly preserved be the plinth upon which we may establish our own I AM Presence. Let us each become a mighty pillar in our own right, collectively creating on Earth an eternal temple in and of the Light that knows no discord, but only Love.

Daye Proffit
February 2015
Laguna Beach, California

*Lady Master Pearl*

## *Esotericism in the West*

The great beings who once lived on Earth and who, through great sacrifice, self-purification, and meditation raised themselves into a higher dimension, are known today as Ascended Masters.[1] In 1875 these Masters inspired Madame Helena Petrovna Blavatsky to start the Theosophical Society for the purpose of making known the great secrets of human evolution that had long been hidden in the Far East. After the death of Madame Blavatsky, the organization continued under the direction of Annie Besant, Henry Steel Olcott, and William Quan Judge. Even with the continuing guidance of the Masters, there is still the impossibility of conveying higher dimensional truth in two-dimensional words, so it is always inevitable that disagreements arise. Many members withdrew over those disagreements and started their own organizations. Some of these were, William Quan Judge, who started the American Theosophical Society; Alice Bailey, who started the Arcane School; Rudolph Steiner, who started the Anthroposophical Society; and Max Heindel, who started the Rosicrucian Fellowship.

---

1   Ascended Master is a term probably coined by Baird T. Spalding around 1924, popularized by Godfre Ray King in the 1930s. The process of consciously dissolving the physical form was well known in Tibet as *jalus*. At this time the human soul, the Higher Mental Body, merges with the Rainbow Body, the I AM Presence, or in Sanskrit, *atman*.

In 1914, Joseph S. Benner broke with the Theosophical tradition that focused on the Masters, and spoke in his book, *The Impersonal Life*, about the need to focus on one's own God Presence prior to Masters and Gurus, and he taught how to invoke that Higher Self through meditation on the I AM.

In 1924, Baird T. Spalding published *Life and Teachings of the Masters of the Far East*, a novel that further popularized the understanding of the Christ Consciousness as existing independent from the person of Jesus Christ, a Consciousness that could be invoked by meditating on the I AM. His books also popularized the understanding of the Ascended Masters, whose activity in the Theosophical literature had remained somewhat obscure.

In 1929, Jiddu Krishnamurti, who had been raised by Annie Besant and the Theosophical Society to be the next World Teacher (a manifestation of the Christ Consciousness known as the Maitreya), renounced that role and proclaimed that people needed to work out their own salvation rather than rely on any teacher. He further stated that this process could only be accomplished by self-observation of oneself in relationship to others. His renunciation of their authority threw the Society into chaos, clearing the spiritual ground for the coming of the New Age of individual self-awareness.

In the 1920s, Guy and Edna Ballard (Godfre and Lotus Ray King) were students of William Quan Judge and Baird Spalding, and acquired much of their initial understanding of the Masters and the I AM from them.

In 1928, Manly P. Hall published his monumental book, *The Secret Teachings of All Ages* (H. S. Crocker

Company), which for the first time explained many of the ancient mysteries in a language the uninitiated could understand. [2]

In 1929 the Ascended Master Saint Germain appeared to Guy Ballard on the slopes of Mount Shasta and began giving him direct guidance and instruction. Soon after, the Ballards founded the Saint Germain Foundation. The Ballards later used the names Godfrey and Lotus Ray King.

In the 1930s, Pearl Dorris became Guy Ballard's student, and later his staff member and assistant. Saint Germain appointed her to be director of the I AM Sanctuary of San Francisco.

---

[2] Pearl met Manly P. Hall at his Philosophical Research Society in Los Angeles. When he saw Pearl sitting in the front row at one of his lectures, he abandoned the topic that was scheduled and, looking her in the eye, said, "Tonight I'm going to talk about Saint Germain."

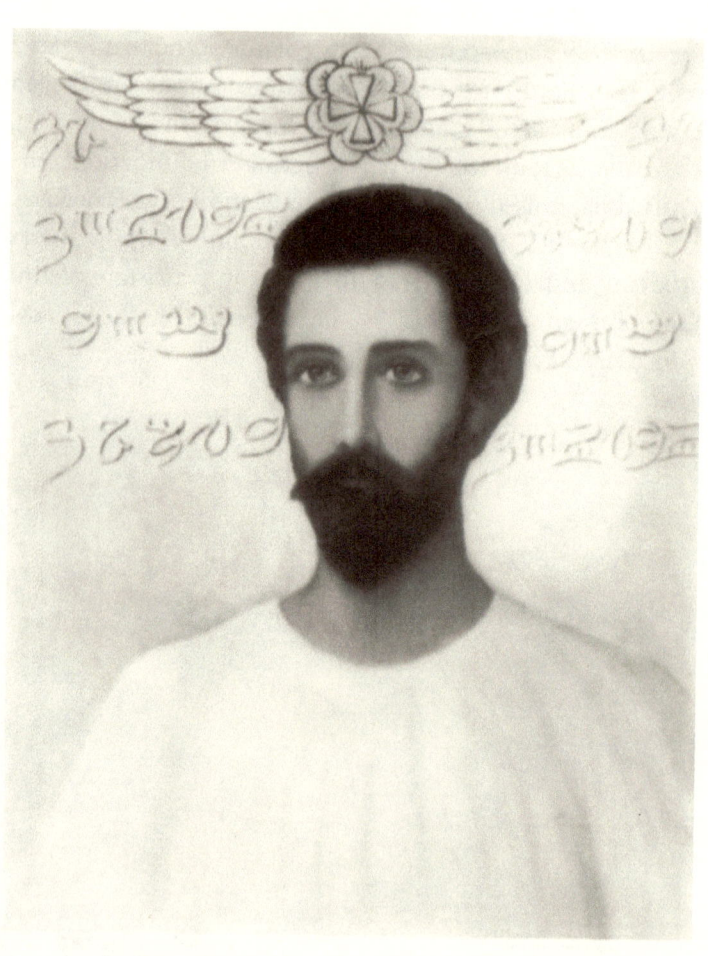

*Ascended Master Saint Germain in his etheric form.*

## *Saint Germain*

"Saint Germain" is the name currently used by that Great Friend who has been working tirelessly for the upliftment of humanity for many ages. He began to appear in many parts of Europe in the early 18th century, using various names such as Count Ragoczy, Comte Soltikoff, and Count Weldone, in addition to le Comte de Saint Germain, depending on the work required. He was well known among the royalty and intelligencia, and his appearances, some of which took place simultaneously in cities as widely separated as Paris and Saint Petersburg, were noted in the diaries of many who were present at that time. During a period of well over a hundred years, he always seemed to be a handsome young man, simply yet elegantly attired, and with vast material resources. No one ever saw him eat or drink, and when it suited him, he was known to vanish without a trace.

Once again, he began to assert his uplifting influence in the late 19th century during the early years of the Theosophical Society. He continues to guide the unfoldment of the new race of advanced beings, actively transmitting the ancient wisdom in a more modern form to all who are receptive.

Saint Germain's great love is in promoting the understanding of the I AM Presence.

*Lady Master Pearl*

## *The I AM Presence*

The I AM Presence is the individualized God Presence from which each person emanates. Called the *Atman* in India, or the *Dharmakaya* by Buddhists, or the Monad by esotericists, It is the Sun-like Individual Source that projects a stream of life force into the physical body. It animates the heart, lungs, mind, and nervous system. Although the tangible feeling It produces in the chest is frequently called the Heart Center, It is actually anchored near the thymus gland, behind the sternum. This Presence is a Flame like the pilot light of a gas stove, invisible until activated. It is the center of the Self. The individual I AM Presence is a fractal of God—all that God is, It is also. When you feel Its Presence, and say the words "I AM," you call It into action, qualified by whatever thought, feeling, or word is in your Consciousness.

*Lady Master Pearl*

# *Preface*

*Om Mani Padme Hung*
(The Jewel in the heart of the Lotus)
-Mantra of *Chenrezig,* Tibetan Lord of Compassion

Although she seemed like an ordinary woman, perhaps your grandmother, people came from all over the world to sit with Pearl in her living room. She had been an associate of Guy Ballard in the 1930s, but rather than continue to give the ancient esoteric teachings of the Masters academically, as they had been taught since the days of the Theosophical Society, she transmitted the reality of God directly heart to heart. After this initiation, you could feel your own I AM Presence, as well as the presence of the Ascended Masters. All you wanted then was to be like those Masters, and Pearl taught that path by her own example.

In 1972, the Masters began sending their students to her. Without warning, many began showing up at her door, having heard of her only by word of mouth. There was no Internet then, yet for the next 18 years, and until her death in 1990, over 12,000 people visited her in Mount Shasta, and through that contact awakened to their own Divinity.

Her small house was at the end of the road, hidden behind a dense hedge. Never wanting to be a teacher, here she and her husband, Jerry, cherished their peace and seclusion. Despite her personal wishes, the Masters began sending people to her as their representative. In her presence your energy was accelerated by those Great Ones—who raised many into the consciousness of their own God Self, the I AM Presence—after which you were never the same.

She had in her heart that illuminated jewel of consciousness, which in Christian literature is called the Pearl of Great Price (Matthew 13:45-46). In the Far East it is called *the Jewel in the Lotus.* Pearl had the ability to transmit that awareness, for which people sought her out, often beginning to arrive at 8 in the morning, and the last one leaving at 10 at night. No request was too insignificant for her, for whether someone sought contact with the Masters or needed help with a relationship, she was always there like a mother. Although she never asked for payment, she would sometimes find checks tucked between the pages of books. Or, people would bring her flowers, crystals, and other tokens of their appreciation. Although her teachings were given freely, her husband, Jerry, worked at the desk of a local motel to make that generosity possible.

I am writing about Pearl now in the hope that others may be inspired by her story and receive the same knowledge of the Inner Presence that was bestowed on me. The Master Saint Germain sent me to her in 1973, after I had returned from travels in the Far East. Seeking direction in life, I had gone into the redwood forest north of San Francisco known as Muir Woods. It was there that the miraculous Saint Germain appeared in physical form, and sent me to Mount Shasta to study with Pearl.

Only rarely does one find a being like Pearl who, instead of merely talking about spiritual truth, was a living example of its power in action. Contacting her was a turning point in the lives of many, and marked an evolutionary leap in the esoteric tradition of the West.

Rather than appearing as a guru, starting an organization, or channeling beings from a higher dimension, she was Everywoman who lived in the Consciousness of her Higher Self in the midst of ordinary life.

*Lady Master Pearl*

# 1

## *Mountain Girl*

Pearl grew up as a free spirit in the wide-open spaces of the Rocky Mountains. She was born in the small town of Laporte, nestled in the Cache La Poudre River Valley, six miles west of Fort Collins, Colorado, on October 20th, 1905. She was the last of six children, including four brothers and a sister, of Alice Permale Winters and William Curtis Hock. They were farmers who grew sugar beets, and when she was not in school, she was feeding the chickens or bringing in kindling for the wood stove. When free, she and her beloved dog Queenie, a Collie-German Shepherd mix, were roaming the mountains. She didn't realize it then, but their farmhouse was near the Cave of Symbols, the Ascended Master Retreat spoken of in *Unveiled Mysteries*.[3] This came to light when, years later, she met the book's author, Godfre Ray King. Under his guidance, the Master Saint Germain would eventually appoint her to run the San Francisco I AM Sanctuary.

Their farmhouse in the mountains did not have insulation, so on winter nights she was sent to bed with a hot brick wrapped in a towel, which she placed in the foot of the bed. One winter she got an ear infection and, after running a high fever for several days, found that she

---

3   *Unveiled Mysteries,* by Godfre Ray King (Saint Germain Foundation, 1934).

had lost much of her hearing. Because of this malady that caused many misunderstandings she always felt inferior, as if she were being punished for some wrong. Although she learned to lip read, she could not understand people unless they were facing her. This inability to converse with others led her to turn her attention inward, and she learned to communicate with her Higher Self and receive answers. This ability to receive answers from her God Self often shocked others, and gave her a reputation as somewhat of a seer.

Soon after her brothers and sisters left home, her mother died. At the age of fourteen, she was left alone on the ranch with her father. Without consulting her, one day he abruptly sold the farm and took Pearl to live in Riverside, California, near Los Angeles. Still mourning the loss of her mother, she was further anguished at leaving the peace and serenity of the mountains. Then she was told she had to leave Queenie behind as well. When she arrived in the crowded plains of Southern California, she went into shock and lost consciousness. She lay in a coma for seven days, and it was thought that she would die. However, during these seven days that her body was inert, she was conscious out of the body, and was shown by the Masters many of her past lives.

She saw that in one life she had failed the mission the Masters had given her, and that her present sense of inferiority was not so much from hearing loss, but from her disobedience in that past life. She saw that she had been a priestess of an Atlantean temple, responsible for teaching young girls how to be virtuous and accomplished women. She had fallen in love with one of the guards, who she didn't realize was her Twin Ray.[4] When it was discovered they had broken their vow of celibacy, the resulting scandal led to the downfall of that temple. That civilization, whose eastern edge was in the area of present day San Francisco, was ended by a great earthquake.

In a more recent lifetime, she had again met her Twin Ray in America in the eighteen hundreds, and again fallen in love. When he married another woman, she had died of a broken heart, again at the age of fourteen. Now at that same age, she had the choice of leaving her body once more, or of remaining to heal that karmic wound and redeem herself. She could once again become a spiritual beacon, and achieve Liberation, Mastery, and the Ascension.

Deciding to stay in embodiment, she was shown the meaning of her name, Pearl, which would always remind her of her lesson. She was like an oyster trying to protect itself from an irritating grain of sand by secreting a liquid around the grain, and eventually forming a pearl. The liquid was the love she would need to enfold and heal the irritation

---

[4] Twin Rays are the dual aspects of a God Flame that has separated into the feminine and masculine aspect for the purpose of learning certain life lessons. Once human evolution is complete, these aspects can again reunite. Not all beings undergo this separation. It is fruitless to search for one's Twin Ray, as the first work is to purify oneself and become conscious of one's own Ray from the I AM Presence. Soul Mates are beings who have worked together in past lifetimes, but are not necessarily Twin Rays.

of her past failures, and that would become a pearl. It was that pearl people would sense—*the jewel in the lotus*—that would enable them to heal their own hearts.

## 2

## *A Mysterious Woman Appears*

The first spiritual teaching Pearl received came to her in the form of the mysterious appearance of a book during her last year of high school. She had begun to learn to drive. One day she failed to let out the clutch in time, and the car bumped into the back of the garage. When she got out to see if she had caused any damage, she noticed a book in the rafters overhead. That was strange, as they hadn't brought any books with them. Getting a ladder, she found that the book was *Your Forces and How to Use Them*, by Christian Larson.[5] Flipping open its pages, she read,

> *The "I AM" is the ruling principle in man, the center and source of individuality, the originator of everything that takes place in man, and that primary something to which all other things in human nature are secondary.*

She took the book inside, and as she read she found that it resonated with what she had already discovered on her own, that there is a presence within one known as the "I AM," and when one is in touch with that force and consciousness, miracles occur. Even as a young

---

[5] *Your Forces and How to Use Them*, by Christian D. Larson (The New Literature Publishing Company, 1912).

girl in the Rocky Mountains, she discovered that when she turned her attention inward she could often see into the future, know what people were thinking, and communicate with animals. The farmers would often consult her, as she knew when the weather would change and when they should harvest their crops. Whenever she turned her attention inward, she could feel that Presence in the center of her chest respond. Larson said that was God, so she began meditating on this Presence, without telling a soul.

Pearl graduated from Riverside High School, then in 1924 moved to Los Angeles. Her desire was to continue her spiritual studies, but needing to earn a living she decided to become a secretary, and enrolled in Hills Business College. After class, however, she would go to the L. A. County Library and search for more spiritual books. One day she was browsing through the stacks, and a beautiful woman came up to her and placed a book on the shelf beside her. Nodding down at it, she communicated telepathically, "I think this is the book you're looking for."

When she picked it up she saw it was another book by Christian Larson. She was going to thank the woman for pointing it out to her, but the woman had disappeared. Opening the book she read,

> *When we have been within the pearly gates of the cosmic world, even but for a moment, life is not the same any more; life is no longer mere existence but a sacred something that we hold too precious to even mention in spoken words.*

*You must act, not as a body, not as a personality, not as a mind, but as the **"I AM,"** and the more fully you recognize the lofty position of the **"I AM"** the greater becomes your power to control and direct all other things that you may possess.*[6]

---

[6] *On the Heights,* by Christian D. Larson (The Progress Company, 1908).

*Pearl Dorris, circa 1925.*

# 3

## *First Job, First Man*

Pearl continued to read Larson's books and apply his teachings. Her attention became more and more focused within, on the God Flame near her heart, yet in 1935 she still managed to graduate from business college. In search of a job, and with barely enough money for bus fare, she moved to San Francisco. She walked up and down the hills, going into office after office, but no one hired her. Things went from bad to worse when she tripped on a staircase and hurt her big toe. In despair, she sat down on the steps and turned her attention inward. She prayed to her Higher Self for assistance,

*Beloved I AM Presence come forth!*

As she then limped into the street, she noticed that she was in front of a doctor's office and thought, "Maybe they need a secretary?"

The doctor's wife, who ran the office, said they didn't need anyone. Pearl turned to leave, and as she limped toward the door, the woman asked what was wrong. Pearl told her, and the woman offered to take her to see the doctor.

"But, I don't have any money," Pearl confessed.

The woman smiled and, touched by Pearl's simplicity, said, "Don't worry about that."

In a moment the doctor could see that the toe was broken, and applied a splint. However, when they saw that Pearl could hardly walk, they said, "You'd better come home with us. We have a spare room. We don't need a secretary, but we have a side business selling cold cream. You could pay for the room by packing cold cream in jars. Would you like that?"

"Oh, yes," Pearl agreed, as she didn't even have money for her next meal. Their offer seemed an answer to her prayer. She felt that stubbing her toe had been due to her stubbornness, showing her that she had been relying too much on her human will. Only after injuring herself and surrendering to the Divine, did the plan unfold. The doctor and his wife were kind to her. The job didn't require much of her time, and soon she found a second job as a typist with F. W. Woolworth & Company.

One day her boss called her into his office and told her to shut the door behind her. Seeing him suffering from the strain of his job, Pearl had been sending love to him and enfolding him in Light. Since she had read the Christian Larson books and learned that Love was the sustaining power of the universe, she tried to emanate that Love to all. Now, however, she was not prepared how that Love was going to come back to her.

Her boss told her to sit down next to him and take a dictation in shorthand, but no sooner had he begun to dictate than he placed his hand on her knee. When she pushed it off, he replaced it. Finally, she stood up and, pointing her finger at him, said, "Don't you ever touch me again."

As she returned to her desk, she realized that she needed to be more discrete with that Love, and learn to withdraw it into herself on occasion. Especially around men, she found that Love was often interpreted sexually, rather than as a natural expression of Divinity.

However, Pearl would soon be brought together with a man toward whom she could express her Love on all levels. As she got used to her new schedule, she decided to take dance classes in the evening. One night she felt an immediate connection with a young man named Sydney. As they dated that summer the bond grew stronger, and feeling they were meant for each other, they soon married. After their honeymoon on the Russian River, they got an apartment together. He worked in the family produce business and she continued at F. W. Woolworth. At last she felt truly established on the Earth as a normal human being, with a job and a loving partner. However, soon the Masters would expand her vision of her true purpose in life.

*Lady Master Pearl*

## 4

### *Good Deed*

As it was during the Depression, with many homeless people in the streets, Pearl and a girlfriend began delivering vegetables to free soup kitchens. She discovered that helping others gave her more joy than doing things for herself, and she spent an increasing amount of time volunteering where needed. Sometimes that service extended to animals, and once even to a plant.

As she was walking home one day, she found a flower growing in a crack in the sidewalk. With so little dirt for its roots, and in constant danger of being trampled, she knew that it would not live long. She returned the next day with a trowel and flowerpot, and dug it up. She brought it home in the flowerpot and set it on her desk under the window, where it would get plenty of light, and she named it Good Deed. Every day she watered it, saying, "I love you, Good Deed," and the plant grew strong and vibrant.

Weeks later, she came home after a hard day's work with a splitting headache. She collapsed at the desk, her head in her arms. As she lay there, feeling more dead than alive, gradually she felt a soothing energy pouring into her, and began to feel better. Finally she raised her head to see the source of the energy, and there in front of her was the plant. She stared at it for a moment in disbelief, thinking, "Plants can't heal."

Yet, she continued to feel love radiating from the plant.

Finally she asked, "Was that you who healed me?"

"Yes," she inwardly heard the plant reply, "I am your Good Deed come back to you."

## 5

### *Saint Germain Appears*

Pearl had just finished her meditation and was sitting in bed staring out the closed window, when a white dove appeared at the pane. It peered in at her intently, and she thought, "That's strange, I wonder what it wants?"

As if in answer to her question, the dove, which at first she had thought was a normal bird, flew through the pane of the closed window, into the room, and landed on her shoulder. It pecked her earlobe, as if wanting to whisper something to her, then said, "You are going to meet a lady, and she will have something important to show you." The bird then pecked her on the lips, like a parting kiss, and flew back out the window.

It was February 20th, 1935, and Pearl was about to meet the Master who would raise her into the consciousness of her own Higher Self and prepare her for her Mission. Using the bird as his Messenger was his humorous way of telling her, "Pay attention!"

Two days later, on George Washington's Birthday, she was invited by Mabel Farrington Gifford, a noted speech therapist and teacher of metaphysics, to drive out to the country and visit her doctor friend and his wife who had first befriended her when she came to San Francisco. Pearl sat alone in the back seat as they drove north on the freeway, when suddenly the same dove appeared at the closed side window of the car and flew through it to again peck Pearl on the cheek.

"This is your lady!" the dove said, and then disappeared.

At that moment Mrs. Gifford turned around and smiled. When they reached the cabin, Mrs. Gifford said, "Pearl, I have something to show you." She asked Pearl to sit at the table, and placed before her a copy of a beautiful green book. Stamped in gold, the title said *Unveiled Mysteries*. As she opened it, the pages fell open to a picture of the Ascended Master Saint Germain, and she received a shock.

"Why, I know him!" she gasped.

"That's impossible, my dear," Mrs. Farrington said, "He's been dead since the seventeen hundreds."

"But I do, I know this man!" Pearl insisted. Turning back to the picture, Saint Germain's face lifted off the page and, coming to life, he winked at her. Inwardly she heard, "Say nothing, our work is just beginning. We shall meet again soon."

Not long after that, Guy Ballard, the author of *Unveiled Mysteries*, came to San Francisco to give teachings. He was also known by his pen name, Godfre Ray King, and was the founder of the Saint Germain Foundation. Eager to meet him, Pearl and Sydney went to the auditorium. No sooner had they entered than two women approached Pearl and said, "Oh, dear, you look like an angel. You are the kind of young person we are looking for to carry the Light. Would you help us by giving out these brochures?"

Always looking for ways to serve, she gladly took a stack of the brochures and began handing them out to people as they arrived. Soon Godfre took the stage, and as he began talking, a powerful energy and consciousness filled the room. She knew at that moment that this was her teacher. Although his words were the essence of simplicity, they had a power she had never experienced.

His message was, what you put your attention upon, you become. If you put your attention on the Light, you become Light. If you put your attention on Love, you become Love. By your thoughts, words, and feelings, you guide your attention; and by the command, "I AM," you call your own God Consciousness forth to bring into being whatever you have thought. When thought and feeling are merged, the spoken word manifests as reality. One can invoke the great Masters the same way, simply by dwelling on the Master and saying, "I AM the presence of Master…."

When she got back to her apartment that night she decided to try what Godfre had taught. She would try to invoke a Master. As she stood in the middle of the floor, arms outstretched, she said,

*"I AM the presence of Jesus the Christ!"*

Suddenly, what seemed to her to be a living, breathing man stood before her, arms outstretched. Terrified, Pearl ran into the bedroom and locked the door. She phoned a lady she had met at the Saint Germain Foundation and pleaded, "There's a man in my apartment!"

"How did he get in?" the woman asked, skeptically.

After Pearl explained what she had done, the woman said, "Go and see if he's still there. If you don't come back in a minute, I will call the police."

Pearl checked the whole apartment, but found it empty. It was then that she realized the power of her attention to bring things into manifestation, but she also realized that she had a lot of fear she needed to dissolve before she could work with the Masters.

Years later in Mount Shasta, she would smile when people told her their stories of how a Master had appeared and they had been struck with fear. "That is why they don't appear more often," she would say, "for most people are not ready for such energy. Their appearance amplifies everything in your world, so before you can be in their presence, first you need to purify yourself."

# 6

## *Experiencing an Ascended Master*

Once Pearl had felt the energy of the Ascended Masters that filled the room when Godfre spoke, she was firmly convinced of their reality and wanted to be a part of that activity as much as possible. That first night she drew the immediate attention of the Ballards, for her purity and innocence radiated from her. They became like a family, and she began helping organize and present Godfre's teachings whenever possible.

These were not inspirational channelings of someone trying to give the message they imagined a particular being would give, but were actual appearances initiated by various Ascended Beings. Godfre would not know who, if anyone, was going to come forth. As the time came to address the audience, he began to feel the energy of a particular Master, which would increase as he began to speak. Then, the Master would begin to impress his mind on Godfre's, until they were one in consciousness. At the same time they would charge their consciousness into the Higher Mental Bodies of everyone present. Although the message was often simple, the spiritual radiation that filled the room was a transcendent emanation that raised all there into the Ascended Master Consciousness.

One night after a discourse by Mighty Victory, when everyone had left the auditorium, Pearl stayed behind to put everything away. She was trying to understand where the energy came from, Godfre or the Masters? As no one was around, she decided to go onstage and experiment. She climbed the steps and walked onstage to the exact spot where Godfre had stood at the microphone, and imitated Godfre by affirming,[7]

*I AM the presence of Mighty Victory!*

A bolt of light shot through her that knocked her against the curtain at the back of the stage, where she collapsed. The accumulated energy of Victory that was still charged into that location had been discharged by Pearl's command. Now she understood that these Masters were not a figment of Godfre's imagination, or astral beings floating around in the atmosphere, but real Beings of tremendous power. It did not surprise her later when she learned that Victory was a being who, through many lifetimes, had never known defeat, and is now available to assist all who are sincere in their efforts to benefit others.

Never again did she say a Master's name lightly, for she now knew that they stood ready to leap forth at the sound of their name. One needed only to turn to one's heart and say the command. She soon had the opportunity to call a Master into action.

Pearl was walking down the sidewalk at night, on her way home to her apartment on Geary Street, when a car screeched to a stop beside her. Two evil looking men peered

---

7   The terms Affirmation and Decree are used somewhat interchangeably; however, a Decree is usually done with more energy.

out the window at her, and her blood ran cold. There had been a number of kidnappings in the City lately, where young women disappeared and were never seen again. Now her fear was confirmed when she heard the driver say to the other man, "Go get her!" The side door opened, and as the unshaven man lurched toward her, she called out, "Saint Germain, come forth!"

Suddenly, the man stopped in his tracks and slid back in the car. Turning around, Pearl saw that standing behind her was a tall, well-built policeman.

"Jesus, the cops!" shouted the driver, and the car squealed away in a cloud of burnt rubber.

"Well, you are timely," Pearl said, recovering her composure, "I don't think those men had good intentions. I would appreciate it if you walk me home."

The handsome police officer smiled and said, "Don't worry, they won't be back."

"But, I only live on the next block."

"I said, they will not be back," he said, firmly. "You will be all right now."

"Well, he's not very cooperative," she thought, and turned to walk the remaining block to her apartment. However, another wave of fear ran through her, and she turned around to beg the officer once more to accompany her, but the sidewalk was empty. He had simply disappeared. "That's peculiar," she thought, and walked on alone, soon reaching home safely.

Later, when she was on the staff of the Saint Germain Foundation, she complained to Godfre that the Masters never helped her the way they did him. Suddenly her inner sight opened, and she saw the amused face of Saint

*Lady Master Pearl*

Germain smiling at her, and he said, "You mean like that night on Geary Street, Pearl?" Then he named two other occasions when he had helped her without her being aware.

# 7

## *Saving a City and Bridge*

Pearl learned gradually to obey the inner feeling in her heart before honoring outer, human commitments.

One day Pearl and two other I AM students were about to depart for an important class by Godfre at the sanctuary, when all three felt the strong impulse to go in the opposite direction. They kept following that inner feeling until they found themselves at the westernmost extreme of San Francisco. They stood on a promontory overlooking the Sutro Baths and the Pacific Ocean. Dark clouds that billowed toward the City turned the sky an inky black and obscured the setting sun. Pearl felt an ominous foreboding, as of some impending disaster, and she and her friends called the Masters into action. As the three of them stood on the headland, they decreed,

> *Mighty I AM Presence and Great Host of Ascended Masters, come forth now and dissolve and consume this force!*
>
> *Archangel Michael and Legions of Blue Flame, blaze your Blue Lightning through this situation now!*
>
> *Saint Germain, come forth and dissolve all negative energy now by the power of the Violet Consuming Flame!*

Remaining in harmony, and focused on the Inner God Presence, they called other Masters into action as well, and within a half hour the clouds had dissolved and the fear of impending doom lifted. Feeling a sense of relief, they now headed back across town to the I AM Sanctuary at 133 Powell Street, where the class had begun. Not wanting to disturb the dictation in progress, they entered the auditorium quietly; but at that moment Godfre looked toward them and said, "Saint Germain wishes to thank these students who just averted a cataclysm and saved this city from a grave disaster. Thank you for your obedience to your own Mighty I AM Presence!"

In 1937 Pearl met a lady from New York's high society, Dr. Mary Francine Watson, toward whom many of the students showed disdain. They felt that because of her elegant clothes and refined manner she couldn't possibly be close to the Masters. However, appearances meant little to Pearl, as she felt the woman's inner purity. One day the New Yorker took Pearl to her apartment and showed her a handful of yellow diamonds that had been given to her by Saint Germain. It was because of stones like these that Yellowstone Park had received its name, and Saint Germain explained to her that these stones, though uncut, emanated a certain energy the Masters could expand to produce a blessing wherever the Masters directed her to place them.

Out of all the I AM students, Saint Germain told her to take only Pearl, and to go to the site where the foundation of the Golden Gate Bridge was under construction. Numerous accidents and fatalities had caused delays, and the Master said that this dangerous condition resulted from the destructive energies from a previous civilization that were still trapped at that location.

Dr. Watson put half the diamonds in Pearl's hands, and as they stood there on Fort Point, a great hierarchy of Angels and Ascended Masters descended, beaming rays of Light through the yellow stones and downward into the earth. Almost overpowered, Pearl struggled to stay present in her body. Her inner sight showed her many discarnate beings trapped there in the astral plane, now being freed. These beings had caused a number of bridge workers to fall to their deaths. After this service by these two women, the negative condition was eliminated, and the bridge construction proceeded more safely.

Soon after, Dr. Watson departed. She took the yellow diamonds to South America under Saint Germain's direction. He told her to place them in certain tunnels in the Andes Mountains where discarnate entities from previous civilizations were trapped. He told her to leave the diamonds, so that after the astral entities were removed, the Masters could direct healing currents of energy into the Earth.

*Lady Master Pearl*

## 8

## *A Master's Request*

Realizing that Pearl was under the guidance of the Masters, Godfre soon invited her to become part of his staff that directed the Saint Germain Foundation. One day in 1938, soon after her thirty-third birthday, Godfre handed Pearl a letter that had been dictated by Saint Germain. It was his wish that she be appointed to lead the I AM Sanctuary of San Francisco. Saint Germain knew how shy she was and how strong her resistance to accepting this position of authority would be, so had felt it was necessary to issue her this direct request. Being younger than most of the members, some of whom had long affiliations with the Rosicrucian Order and the Theosophical Society, she felt that no one would take her seriously. Also, her hearing deficit still continued to cause misunderstandings in her interaction with others; so she told Godfre that she couldn't possibly accept the offer.

After a sleepless night, she realized that she could not turn down a request by Saint Germain, especially since he had gone to the trouble of dictating the request, so she told Godfre she would serve in any way required. Since this new responsibility would require most of her time, she quit her job at Woolworth and Company, without any idea how she and Sydney were going to pay the rent. Since her husband was not making much money in the produce business, their financial situation was precarious.

Gradually some of the wealthier I AM students began to learn of their situation, and began to make contributions to support Pearl in her service.

One day she was working at her desk in the office, when a stranger entered and began asking questions about the I AM teachings. When he asked if he could see the sanctuary, she said that they normally did not admit non-students, but she would be happy to show it to him. It was an elegant, pure white room with a large picture of Jesus and Saint Germain on either side of the shrine, and a crystal vase in the center that served as a focus of the Unfed Flame.[8]

"What is the Unfed Flame?" he asked, looking intently into her eyes.

"It is symbolic of the focus of Light from the I AM Presence that is anchored in the heart of every person. Every person is sustained by his or her own Unfed Flame."

"And you believe that?" he asked, pointedly.

"Why, yes, I do."

Then in a gentle voice, but one which nevertheless carried great authority, he said, "When you have raised your energy from your lower centers to the level of your

---

[8] The Unfed Flame is the focus of the I AM Presence in the center of one's chest near the thymus gland, that sustains life. In previous Golden Ages, external flames were established in temples by great Masters as reminders of the Inner Flame, and as a blessing to society. A spiritual flame can be invoked by any individual in a shrine, home, or other location.

heart, then you will BE the Unfed Flame, and then your true work will begin."

He bowed courteously, thanked her for her time, and walked to the door and down the steps. Pearl walked back to the office and sat down at her desk. "That's strange," she thought. "Why did he pretend to know nothing about spirituality, and then act as if he knew what I needed to work on?" She thought his remark a bit insolent. At that moment she felt a rush of light-hearted energy that could only come from one source, and she realized who the stranger had been: not an ordinary curiosity seeker stumbling in off the street, but the Master Saint Germain himself.

After a great deal of thought about the meaning of his comment, she realized that she and Sydney needed to raise their energy rather than expending it through indulging in sexual activity. Sydney was resistant, but gradually they moved into a celibate relationship. A couple of generations later they might have received tantric instruction in how to conserve the life force rather than repress it, but in the 1930s the only qualified teachers of that science of rejuvenation were probably in China, India, and Tibet.[9]

---

9   *Tantra* (Sanskrit: continuity) is the science of using meditation, ritual, and visualization to realize the transcendental nature of reality in the appearance world of mundane reality. Hence, all aspects of daily life, including relationship, can be used as spiritual tools for liberation from delusion. The ancient Buddhist *Tantrikas* and Chinese Taoists practiced various methods to conserve and transmute sexual energy into spiritual.

*Godfre and Lotus in the 1930s.*

## 9

### *Incurring the Wrath of Beloved Mama*

Although Godfre and Lotus had welcomed Pearl into their Saint Germain Foundation "family" wholeheartedly, gradually Pearl began to feel that Mrs. Ballard, whom everyone called "Beloved Mama," resented Pearl's spiritual affinity with Godfre. She tried to ignore the hostility directed at her, and continue to believe that both "Messengers" were infallible; however she began to see things that could no longer be ignored.

Pearl had learned to sew from her mother and made all her own clothes. One day she saw some emerald-colored fabric, which she purchased and made into a stylish cape. A few days later she sat in the front row of the auditorium, sporting her new cape. When Mrs. Ballard took the stage to make announcements and saw the cape, her eyes flashed with displeasure. The next day an announcement was issued, "Students of the Saint Germain Foundation are forbidden to wear capes."

However, a week later Mrs. Ballard appeared on stage wearing a cape much like Pearl's. This was one of the first of many rulings Mrs. Ballard would make as to how students were to live their lives. Eventually she went so far as to dictate what color clothes students must wear each day, and to ban swimming and attending the cinema.

Shortly after the cape incident, Pearl learned there was to be a gala event called Breakfast With the Master, to which Saint Germain had been invited. It was to be held at the elegant Sir Francis Drake Hotel, between Nob Hill and the I AM Sanctuary, and admission was by invitation only. When Pearl did not receive an invitation, she thought that, among the three hundred invitations, hers must have been lost. Contacting Mrs. Ballard's staff, she was told that everything was perfect and that Mrs. Ballard herself had handled the guest list. In shock, she went to the hotel the morning of the breakfast and sat in the lobby as the guests arrived. They had set a place for Saint Germain at the head of the table, and although they weren't sure if he would attend in his physical form, they knew that he would be present, at least in his higher form.

Still hopeful, Pearl asked one of her friends to see if there wasn't an invitation set aside for her, but the woman returned saying that there wasn't one. Disconsolate, she sat at a small desk on the landing outside the banquet hall in case she was invited in at the last moment. However, the breakfast began, and she could hear the clatter of dishes as everyone was served. Then came the prayers and invocation to the Master.

"Saint Germain!" Pearl pleaded inwardly, "What have I done wrong? Please send someone here right now to explain where I have erred."

As if in answer to her prayer, the double doors of the banquet hall opened and Godfre emerged. He came straight over and sat down at the table directly across from her. Leaning over, he looked into her eyes and, taking both her hands in his, said, "You have it, dear heart. Don't ever lose it."

A charge of love filled the space between them. Then

he rose and said, apologetically, "I have to get back now, before Mama discovers I'm gone. Bless you, dear heart."

As Godfre disappeared, Pearl felt that, indeed, there had been no mistake. She had received a greater blessing this way than if she had attended the breakfast, and she departed with the God Flame blazing in her heart.

*Lady Master Pearl*

## 10

## *Meeting of the Twin Rays*

Pearl had been taking flying lessons. She found that the astral plane composed of human thoughts and emotions did not extend over eight thousand feet above the ground, and that it was much easier to still the mind at those altitudes, one of the reasons many yogis dwell in high mountains. It also facilitated her ability to travel consciously in her Higher Mental Body.[10] She used to take the Ballards' son, Donald, flying with her, as he loved the excitement.[11]

One day while flying in 1939, she experienced this enhanced ability to travel consciously in her Higher Mental Body. Without understanding what was happening, she found herself standing in the control room of a radio station. Two men with knives were advancing on the announcer, toward whom she felt a great sense of protection, and one of

---

10  The lifestream of every individual has bodies on different levels of existence, all animated by the same ray of light (Silver Cord) from the I AM Presence. In Buddhism, these bodies are called the *Nirmanakaya*, physical body; *Sambhogakaya*, mental body; and *Dharmakaya*, I AM Presence.

11  Donald Ballard resigned from the I AM Activity in 1957. He apparently wrote a scathing criticism of the Saint Germain Foundation, but before it was published it seems that they managed to locate and destroy most of the copies of the manuscript.

them said to him, "This will teach you to be a strike-breaker!"

Suddenly they saw Pearl standing there, and one of them said, "Where did she come from? Let's get out of here," and they ran out the back door. Then Pearl was back in her physical body. She didn't know where that drama had occurred, although she was soon to find out.

Not long after that, Godfre told Pearl that there was going to be a class in Philadelphia, and requested that she attend. She said, "Gladly," but secretly wondered how she would get the money. She turned her thoughts to Saint Germain, and soon her prayers were answered by a number of the I AM students pitching in to buy her a plane ticket and a suitable wardrobe. She seemed to have everything she needed except a handbag. However, on arrival at the airport, the lady who drove her there gave her an exquisite handbag that matched her new dress perfectly. Entering the terminal, she went to a table to switch the contents from her old purse, and found that the new one was full of money.

She would need that cash when she arrived in Philadelphia, for she found that the class had been moved to Washington, DC, and she had to take a train immediately. She arrived at Hotel Washington on 15th Street, just a block from the White House, and when she went to the front desk to ask for a room, found that one had already been reserved and paid for adjacent to the Ballards.

As the class began, Pearl was seated in the front row. The Ballards were to be introduced by a former radio announcer from Minneapolis, Bob LeFevre, who was now joining the Ballards' staff. When he came on stage, Pearl was shocked to see the man in the radio station whose life she had saved in her vision. As he began to speak he said, "These I AM teachings are a Pearl of Great Price," and he looked directly at her. At that moment, a beam of light joined their hearts, and Pearl knew that they had work to do together—although what that might be she had no idea. She soon found out that Bob was married, and she was still married to Sydney.

The next day Godfre invited Pearl and Bob to visit Mount Vernon with him, the former home and burial place of George Washington, whom Godfre had been told was one of his former embodiments. As the three of them stood looking at the marble sarcophagus, the Masters poured an energy down through them that not only revealed to Godfre the truth of that embodiment, but also raised him into a higher consciousness. The power was so great that Pearl had to hold on to a wall for support. When Godfre turned around, Pearl saw a light shining from him that she had never seen before, and at that moment she knew he would soon be ascending. In confirmation Godfre nodded and said, "You mustn't tell Mrs. Ballard."

Then he told Pearl and Bob that they were Twin Rays and that the Masters had brought them together for a special work he wanted them to do together. They were told not to reveal that connection to anyone in order not to arouse suspicion and gossip—one of the reasons why the motto of the Great White Brotherhood is:

*To know, to dare, to do, and to be silent!*

That night back at the hotel all the staff of the I AM Activity who were present in Washington gathered in the Ballards' suite. They invoked the Masters and then sat in silent contemplation of the great I AM Presence. As they were sitting in harmony, their beloved Master Saint Germain stepped out of the atmosphere in physical form and greeted them with warmth and friendship. There was no blaze of light or choir of angels. He came as simply another being with the sincere desire to assist humanity. He explained that there were many challenges ahead and that they needed to be on guard against certain dark forces, but that he would be with them.[12] They should visualize a crystal tube of light extending down from their God Self, completely enveloping them in a diamond-like circle of protection. If under attack, they were to call on him, and he would respond. He instructed Pearl that she was to be a courier for the manuscript of discourses the Ascended Masters had given through Godfre, and that instead of flying back to California she was to travel by bus. His message completed, he bowed with a grace that would have suited the court of France a century before, and suddenly he was gone. In the charged silence, their hearts were filled with gratitude at the blessing of his miraculous appearance.[13]

---

12  Black magicians on the astral plane attempt to stop the expansion of the light. The Ascended Masters frequently requested the students of the Ballards to make calls to the Ascended Masters to remove these beings from the Earth.

13  Saint Germain, in his Ascended Master body, was a frequent visitor in the courts of Europe during the 1700s, and was known as the Miracle Man of Europe. He was described by Voltaire as "the man who knows everything, and never dies."

# 11

## *A Lady Master to the Rescue*

Clutching the parcel of the manuscript wrapped in brown paper, Pearl boarded the Greyhound bus headed for California. During the night, the bus stopped in pitch darkness far out in the country. She thought it strange that there was no scheduled stop there, but a very attractive lady boarded the bus. She asked Pearl, "May I sit next to you?"

"Well, why don't you sit back there?" Pearl replied, nodding to the rows of vacant seats further back, as she wanted to keep the space beside her vacant.

"But, I prefer this seat," the lady insisted.

"Very well," Pearl said, clearing her coat from the seat, and the lady sat beside her.

Deciding to make the best of having a companion, Pearl tried to strike up a conversation, but the woman ignored her questions and closed her eyes, and Pearl went back to gazing out the window.

A few minutes later, however, her eyes opened in shock. A tractor-trailer that had just passed flipped over in front of them and turned sideway across the road. Sparks were flying as the rig slid down the freeway, and she braced for the inevitable collision. At their speed there was no way the driver could avert a collision, and she was sure they would all be killed. Just then, at the moment before impact, the woman beside her straightened up in her seat, raising her right hand in the air, and the bus rose off the road, went through the wreck, and emerged on the other side. As the bus settled back on the freeway, the woman lowered her hand and leaned back in her seat, and the bus continued on its way as though nothing unusual had happened.

"Did you see that?" Pearl exclaimed to her companion, but the woman only shook her head. Pearl looked around to see others' reaction to this miracle, but none seemed aware of what had happened. Some were asleep, and others reading or talking. Once again Pearl tried to strike up a conversation with the strange woman beside her, but the woman again shook her head, indicating that she preferred silence.

Soon the bus slowed and pulled to the side of the road, again in a dark place in the middle of nowhere. The woman beside her rose, walked up the aisle, and descended the steps, disappearing into the darkness. The door slammed shut, and the bus pulled back out onto the freeway.

Days later the bus pulled into Denver and, leaving her package in the overhead rack, Pearl disembarked. As she went to freshen up, there before her was the woman who had sat beside her several days before. Just as she was about to ask how she got there, the woman approached her and said, "I hope you didn't leave anything valuable on the bus."

Still dazed from the long bus ride, Pearl suddenly remembered the manuscript. Taking the hint, she turned around and headed back toward the bus, but in front of her was an ominous, unshaven man blocking her path. He muttered to himself, "I'll get her, I'll get her, don't you worry, I can do it...."[14]

---

14 Weak minded people or those under the influence

Just then a tall man in a bus driver's uniform walked up to the man, pointed his finger at him, and said in a commanding voice, "Leave! Leave now and don't come back."

"Oh!" the man said, startled, as though waking from a dream. He looked around at what seemed unfamiliar surroundings, and stumbled away.

"He will not bother you again," the driver assured Pearl. "Now, I suggest you return to the bus as soon as possible."

Upon her arrival in Los Angeles several staff members met Pearl at the depot, and drove her to put the manuscript in Godfre's hands. After she told him her adventures, he said, "Who do you suppose that bus driver was? It was our beloved Master."

"And what about that strange woman who sat next to me?" Pearl continued.

"Your namesake."

"Pearl?"

"Yes, the same Lady Master Pearl I wrote about in *The Magic Presence*.[15]

---

of alcohol or drugs can easily be influenced by astral entities and are sometimes brought under hypnotic control by them to do their bidding.

15 *The Magic Presence,* by Godfre Ray King (Saint Germain Press, 1935). There are beings on many levels, including the Cosmic, who embody the Pearl principle and use that name. This is similar to the Tibetan Buddhist understanding that certain individuals are emanations of a particular Deity, e.g., many women may embody the same aspect of the Divine Mother, such as the White, Green, or Red Tara.

*Lady Master Pearl*

## 12

## *Pearl Stirs Up a Firestorm*

Godfre asked Pearl to teach classes at the Sanctuary in his absence. The essence of these I AM teachings is that God is within every human being, and the awareness of that Presence can be strengthened by contemplating the energy and consciousness evoked by the words "I AM." Then, whatever words, thoughts, and feelings you associate with "I AM" will begin to manifest. However, Pearl had begun to notice that many of the students were calling on the Presence as something external, apart from themselves, much in the same way as some religions present God as something external, someone who is "out there." Some students had begun to pray to an artist's rendering of the I AM Presence they had hanging on the wall, addressing it as "Mighty I AM Presence," rather than claiming, "I AM the Presence," and feeling it within themselves. She saw that the Saint Germain Activity was rapidly becoming another religion in which people invoked an external God and external Masters, afraid to search for and claim their own Divinity.

One day she stood in front of the auditorium and felt a wave of shock when she said, "What your attention is upon, you become. What you want, you have to call for. If you want goodness, you have to say 'I AM good.'"

"You can't say that!" some of the staff called out, waving their hands in protest as though she had committed blasphemy.

"I can't say what?" retorted Pearl.

"You can't say that you are good. Haven't you done plenty of bad things? Don't you ever think bad thoughts? Don't you ever get angry?"

"Sure," Pearl shrugged, "but if you don't claim goodness, you will never be good. I am not going out and proclaiming to the world that I am better than anyone, and I am not telling you that, but I am claiming goodness for myself.

"I do not believe we were born sinners, as Christianity says. We were born good. Regardless of how many bad things I may have done, the Love in my heart is good. The Light in the center of my being is good. That Light is wholly pure and perfect, and I am going to claim that perfection and call it forth. I have to start somewhere, and I am starting by saying, 'I AM good.'

"I AM the Presence of God! I AM the Presence of Saint Germain. I AM the Presence of Archangel Michael! Say the name of whatever Master or quality you want to manifest, and then feel that energy as it comes forth."

Soon she was called into the office by some of the leaders, and they said, "Pearl, you have to stop talking like that. You can't claim these things, and we are going to tell Godfre."

"Very well," she said in her feisty manner. "Go ahead and tell him. I'll be glad to hear what he has to say."

Next time Godfre was in San Francisco, Pearl went to

see him. However, Mrs. Ballard was now taking increasing charge over the running of the organization, and made every effort to keep Pearl away from Godfre. However, she knew he had been told how she had been presenting the I AM, and that he would have stopped her if he had disapproved.

As the arguments between Godfre and his wife over the running of the Activity increased, she saw him withdraw more and more, and watched as the more dogmatic elements of the organization began to take control. With sadness, she saw how the discord began to affect his sensitive nervous system and physical health, a situation kept hidden from the students.

*Lady Master Pearl*

## 13

## *The Ascension of Godfre Ray King*

Ever since Pearl had stood beside Godfre at George Washington's tomb and been shown that he would soon be ascending, she had observed him becoming increasingly etheric and removed from earthly conditions. His marriage to his wife, Lotus, never an easy one, became increasingly strained. At staff meetings she would contradict Godfre to his face and have temper tantrums if opposed. Passing by their room, Pearl often heard Lotus berating Godfre, and cringed at his suffering.

At the end of December 1939, they were all staying at the Biltmore Hotel in Los Angeles for the Christmas Class. Godfre had been looking increasingly pale and withdrawn and, knowing that he had been having circulatory problems, it was little surprise to her when on the morning of the 29th she was told that Godfre had died of heart failure early that morning. Shortly after she received the news, the phone in her room rang and she heard the friendly voice of Saint Germain, "Pearl, I want to use you and Bob as my next Messengers of the Activity. I don't know if Lotus will accept, but I am going to try. Will you help me?"

"Of course," Pearl said, "in any way I can."

"Then you will be seeing me shortly. Call Bob and tell him to put his attention on me." Then the phone call ended.

Immediately Pearl phoned Bob's room, and she realized how occupied he was in dealing with the commotion

*Lady Master Pearl*

among the rest of the staff. Godfre had given a number of discourses in which he said that sincere I AM students would never know death, and that he personally would ascend in his physical body. Many were demanding to know now why that had not happened. Not knowing how to deal with this massive contradiction of an important part of their teachings, Mrs. Ballard told the students that Godfre was out of town on business with Saint Germain, until she could think of what to say.

In the midst of this turmoil, Bob was grateful to hear the phone ring and Pearl say, "The Master wants you to take your attention off the outer conditions and focus instead on him."

"Gladly!" Bob replied, relieved.

"We have work to do together," Pearl concluded, and then hung up. As Mrs. Ballard had forbidden the students from wearing black under any circumstances, she had to choose a dress to wear at the funeral. Mrs. Ballard had established the rule that all were expected to wear the color she had determined was associated with the energy of each day of the week. If you didn't have the correct color, white was always acceptable, so Pearl took her white dress out of the closet.

The funeral service was held on the morning of January 1st at their son Donald's home, and all the staff members and Sanctuary leaders from around the country were invited. There were seventy-two in all, and they formed a circle around the coffin, Mrs. Ballard stationed at the head.[16]

---

16   I have given here the description of Godfre's ascension

Beautiful harp and organ music was played, and the students joined together in affirmations for Godfre's ascension. As the ceremony continued, Pearl's inner sight opened, and she saw a Divine Being of Light standing at both the head and foot of the coffin. Rings of angels descended and she began hearing celestial overtones to the earthly music.

Then she saw Godfre, looking more youthful and radiant than she had ever seen, and Saint Germain and Jesus stood on either side of him. These Masters began gradually lifting him from the Earth. As they rose, Godfre's bliss was so ecstatic that he wanted to communicate his joy to the students, but the Masters restrained him. They rose higher into the atmosphere and finally disappeared into the Light.

His physical body was cremated that afternoon, and Mrs. Ballard released a formal announcement to the students that Godfre had ascended under a "new dispensation" that did not require one to actually raise the physical body.[17]

---

    as Pearl described it to me. It is also described similarly in *"I AM" America's Destiny*, by Pearl Diehl and Robert LeFevre (Twin City House, 1940).

17  This was nothing new, as in India it was well understood that higher initiations did not require one to dissolve the physical form, but took place in higher dimensions where the soul (*jiva*) once again reconnects intimately with the I AM Presence (*atman*). Actual Ascension of the physical form has been long practiced by adepts in China, India, and Tibet (Tibetan: *jalus*), in which case the physical constituents of the body are returned

*Lady Master Pearl*

---

consciously to the Source. Liberation (*moksha*), on the other hand, is simply the freedom from the need to re-embody on Earth, which occurs when one has finished one's earthly karma and learned all that one has come into embodiment to learn.

## 14

## *Who is the Next Messenger?*

Of the seventy-two people present at Godfre's funeral, Pearl realized that only a few witnessed what she had seen, and Mrs. Ballard was not one of them. She had remained with face downcast throughout the service, showing no sign of the spiritual illumination that Pearl and a few others felt. On the contrary, Mrs. Ballard seemed preoccupied with the conundrum of Godfre's failure, and to resolve it she finally decided to announce his Ascension.

Realizing that Mrs. Ballard was not as sensitive to the Masters as Godfre, and seeing the many people who felt deceived were cancelling their membership, she wondered if this would lead to the end of the Saint Germain Foundation.

Her question was soon answered in a most remarkable way the next day, when Saint Germain appeared to her and said, "I want to show Mrs. Ballard that I am working through you, and that I want the two of you to be the new Messengers. I am not sure if she will accept it, but I have to try. I want you and Bob to get together and write a book. I will dictate the words to Bob, and you will write down what he says."

Pearl protested that the male and female students were not allowed to visit each other's rooms, especially since both were still married. Nonetheless, she told the Master that she would try to persuade Bob to come to visit her.

*Lady Master Pearl*

As she had expected, he refused, saying that it was against the rules.

"I think I can take care of that, Pearl," Saint Germain said, with a twinkle in his eye.

He told her to open the window, which looked out on the courtyard of the hotel. In a few minutes she saw Bob's window open across the courtyard, eight stories high, and his prone body float across the open space, and into her window. His body came to rest on the carpeted floor in the middle of the room. He seemed to be asleep, but when she knelt beside him and spoke his name, his eyes opened. He looked up into her face and asked, "Where am I?"

"In my room."

"That's impossible!"

"Not to Saint Germain."

She looked into his eyes, and as their gazes met, their past life connections were revealed in an instant, and Bob passed out from the shock. As he revived, and Pearl started to recount what she had seen, he passed out a second time. Next time, as he came to, he held up his hand and said, "Don't say another word!"

Gradually, he moved to a chair and looked around. He saw that he was truly in Pearl's room—and realized that only Saint Germain could have brought him there. He remembered talking with Pearl on the phone, then feeling tired and lying down on the bed. The next thing he knew he was looking up into Pearl's loving eyes. She explained the Master's wish, and he said, "Yes, I have always known that we had work to do together."

The next day Bob was more willing to break the rules,

and he came voluntarily to Pearl's room. She had bought a ream of paper and half a dozen pencils. As they were sitting at the desk, there was a knock at the door, and although they were not expecting anyone, they said, "Come in."

To their joy, it was the Master Saint Germain, but appearing as a stylish young man dressed in ordinary clothes. Walking over to Pearl, he said, "Hold out your hand."

Extending her hand as requested, the Master placed his hand a few inches above hers. She felt something hard drop into her open palm, and when he withdrew his hand, she saw that she was holding a huge, flawless amethyst. The gem was a couple of inches long and the square ends were about an inch on a side. He instructed them to take the stone to a jeweler and have it cut in half, and to make two identical rings of 24 carat gold. Each ring was to have a torch on each side to represent their roles as intended torchbearers of Light.[18] He also said that the stone represented their unity as Twin Rays of the same Divine Presence. Then he said that he would contact them through the amethyst. If they became distracted by worldly concerns, he would send a charge through the rings to get their attention. He told them to be ready, that soon the dictation would begin—and suddenly they were alone.

Almost immediately Bob began receiving a dictation from Saint Germain, and Pearl wrote down what he said. Within a week they had the manuscript of a small book, which was to be called *"I AM" America's Destiny*. Just as

---

18  A drawing of this ring by the well-known stained glass artist Zenon Michalak is in Pearl's book *Step by Step We Climb* (M. S. Princess, 1978).

they were wondering where to get the money to print the book, one of the students approached Pearl and asked if she needed anything. He was happy to write a check for the printing of ten thousand copies—which were to go out to the students. In an amazingly short time they had a proof copy in their hands, and Pearl was instructed to present it to Mrs. Ballard.

With great trepidation Pearl approached "Beloved Mama" and, placing the book in her hand, said, "The Master Saint Germain dictated this book to Bob and me, and told us to give the first copy to you."

Looking at the book that Pearl had just placed in her hands, Mrs. Ballard became livid. Trembling with rage, she threw it across the room. "The Masters don't come to anyone but me!" she shouted, and stormed out of the room.

Pearl and Bob met back at her room, and Saint Germain communicated mentally to both of them, "It is as I feared, but we needed to try. Now I will begin to shut down the Activity, and give my teachings through other avenues. I want the two of you to resign, and await further instructions."

Pearl returned to San Francisco, and at the next group meeting in the auditorium she announced to the student body, "I have received guidance to resign, not only as director of this Sanctuary, but also from the Saint Germain Foundation."

There were gasps from the audience, but she went on, "This is my own choice, so don't withdraw from the Activity because of what I am doing. Please follow your own guidance."

However, many students and staff members had already begun to withdraw. Godfre was the one whom Saint Germain had contacted on Mount Shasta and used as a messenger these past ten years. Having seen Mrs. Ballard's emotional outbursts, and feeling lied to about Godfre's Ascension, they did not feel that she had the receptivity to receive dictations from the Masters, nor the stability to lead the Activity.

In retaliation for Pearl's resignation, Mrs. Ballard organized a secret group of her loyal followers. Through the use of powerful decrees, they attempted to remove Pearl from embodiment. She fell ill so suddenly she couldn't even raise her head from the bed. No doctor could diagnose what was wrong, and it seemed that she would soon die. Then, some students discovered what Mrs. Ballard was doing, and they organized a counter group, surrounding Pearl in a circle of protection day and night, and she began to improve. In addition, when Mrs. Ballard found out that she had been discovered, she soon discontinued her efforts.[19]

True to his word, Saint Germain began shutting

---

19 Years later in the 1960s, Mrs. Ballard invited Pearl to visit her at Shasta Springs near Dunsmuir, California, and asked Pearl to rejoin the Saint Germain Foundation. Their numbers had dwindled from an estimated 50,000 down to around 2,500. Pearl said, "I'm sorry, but I could never call you 'Beloved Mama,' the way everyone else does." Mrs. Ballard replied, "That's fine, you wouldn't need to, but I could certainly use your help." Pearl replied, "Thank you, but I have my freedom now, and I intend to keep it."

down the Saint Germain Foundation by directing the U. S. Postal Department to investigate Mrs. Ballard, Donald, and the Foundation, for committing mail fraud. The case was brought to trial in 1942, and Pearl was subpoenaed.

As she sat in the office of the U. S. Attorney General to give her deposition, the Attorney leaned forward and, pointing to a large portrait of Saint Germain leaning against the wall, said, "So, who is this Saint Germain?"

Pearl began to explain the miraculous history of this amazing being, and suddenly the picture seemed to come to life. The Attorney's eyes popped open, and he shouted, "Did you see that?"

He continued to sit for an hour, enthralled by her tales of the Master's exploits, first as the author of the Shakespeare plays during his last human embodiment as Sir Francis Bacon, and then as an Ascended Master in the courts of Europe during the time leading up to the French Revolution. Then Pearl told of some of her own encounters with the Master during her time serving the Ballards.

However, the jury found Mrs. Ballard guilty of fraud. They did not feel that the spiritual teachings were false (an issue which the Supreme Court decided could not be brought before the court) but they felt that Mrs. Ballard did not believe in her own teachings, and that she was using them purely for financial gain. In 1946 the case was appealed and the verdict reversed on the grounds that no women had been on the jury. The initial finding of fraud, however, damaged the reputation of the Foundation so badly that members left in droves. As Saint Germain had promised, he now began to release his teachings in new forms and through diverse groups.

It was the beginning of the Aquarian Age, and the Ascended Masters began to gather about them those who wished to teach individual self-empowerment by more universal means than group obedience. It was the beginning of an age in which individuals would awaken spontaneously, where teachers and groups would not seek to control their members, but would serve as catalysts to awaken people to the Light within.[20] Under the direction of Saint Germain, one of these new groups began to form around Pearl.[21]

As all spiritual teachings are only approximations of

---

20  Pearl met Krishnamurti in Ojai in the 1940s. After inviting her to his home for tea he later reported to his neighbor, with whom Pearl was staying, "She is one of the few people I've ever met who wanted nothing from me." Annie Besant and the Theosophical Society had raised Krishnamurti to be the next World Teacher, a sort of Messiah, a role that he renounced in 1929. Instead, he said that people needed to work out their own salvation and not rely on someone else. He emphasized that liberation could only be achieved through self-observation, especially in relation to others. This was to become the keynote of the incoming New Age.

21  Other former I AM students who began giving teachings about the Masters around this time and starting their own groups were: Geraldine Innocente (Bridge to Freedom), A. D. K. Luk, and Mark and Elizabeth Prophet (Summit Lighthouse).

truth, and unlimited Consciousness can only be given indirectly through the limited media of words, even a discourse by an Ascended Master is colored by the mind of the one receiving the message. Proof of this is in the countless discrepancies in the teachings of previous Messengers of the Masters, and the disagreements as to what is "true" among many learned Theosophists, supposedly so close to the Masters. These Masters can only work with the tools they have available, no matter how imperfect. Transcendent spiritual truth can only be perceived inwardly, and when explained to others it loses in the outer exposition.[22]

Reading some of Godfre's discourses, Pearl was occasionally puzzled by statements that did not seem to have the same level of truth as the rest of the discourse. As she examined the situation, she realized that the stenographer did not always distinguish between Godfre's personal, off-hand remarks made during gaps, and the words spoken by the Masters. The staff tried to edit these remarks out before publication, but often a few sentences

---

[22] Even though the knowledge of the Ascended Masters came from India, when the great Indian yogi Paramahansa Yogananda came to America to teach the methods by which the inner God Presence could be realized, the Ballards dissuaded their students from practicing yoga and meditation. They said, as the Foundation still maintains, that meditation makes people passive and deprives them of their will to act. It was not until Pearl began teaching, that a way was shown to balance the inner and outer aspects of spirituality in the daily practice of Mastery.

slipped through. This was later pointed out to her by Sunny Widell, a former editor at the well-known spiritual book publisher, DeVorss and Company.[23]

She also wondered why the Foreword to both *Unveiled Mysteries* and *The Magic Presence* said that everything in the books took place on the physical plane, for she knew that most of Godfre's experiences portrayed in those books took place out of the body, either on the etheric level or in dreams. He wrote about visits to Paris and the Far East, yet she knew that he had never physically been out of the United States; in fact, he had never owned a passport.

Eventually, she realized that Mr. and Mrs. Ballard had collaborated on the books, and, wanting people to believe the truth of the Laws of Life portrayed, had said that all Godfre's experiences were real, physical plane occurrences. Even though many of these experiences were fictionalized, they portrayed the working of Spiritual Law and were conduits of the radiation of the Masters. Until the end of her life, she still regarded *Unveiled Mysteries* and *The Magic Presence* as her favorite books.

Even when Pearl met Baird T. Spalding, the author of *Life and Teachings of the Masters of the Far East*, the fifth volume of which Sunny was then editing, she discovered that his books also were about inner experiences he had had prior to leaving the United States. Only years later,

---

[23] Later, Sunny Widell moved to Mount Shasta, where I worked with her briefly, editing Pearl's discourses. A description of the turmoil that ensued is in *Adventures of a Western Mystic, Part I: Apprentice to the Masters* (Church of the Seven Rays, 2010).

and at the request of his publisher who wanted to generate publicity, did he lead a group to India. Then, none of the members of that "Spalding Expedition" saw any of the Masters he had so beautifully written about in his novels.[24]

---

24 When Pearl began to teach almost thirty years later, she was hesitant to talk about the true nature of Godfre's books, for she didn't want to disappoint those who had read them and came to her filled with enthusiasm. Most people's experiences on the spiritual path are usually much less dramatic than the adventures about which they have read. However, Pearl never questioned some of Godfre's statements, which later turned out to be his personal beliefs rather than direct revelation. One of these was his propagation of "George Washington's Vision," a fictional account of the future of America, written by a journalist about 80 years after it was purported to have been written. See: www.snopes.com/history/american/vision.asp.

## 15

## *Romance, Marriage, and Divorce*

After 1940, and under Saint Germain's direction, a group of those who had withdrawn from the Saint Germain Foundation began to gather around Pearl. They met at her apartment in San Francisco near the Presidio. However, as her marriage to Sydney was drawing to a close, she accepted an invitation to live on a fruit ranch in Santa Rosa, and the group meetings relocated. Pearl had taken seriously Saint Germain's instruction to raise all her energy to her heart, a move toward celibacy that Sydney found difficult to accept. Little did any of them realize the shuffle of partners that Saint Germain was about to orchestrate.

A core group that varied between twelve to twenty former I AM students, including Bob, Sunny, and a man named Jerome "Jerry" Dorris, would meet at the ranch every other week.[25] In dictating *"I AM" America's Destiny*, Saint Germain had trained Pearl and Bob to work together

---

25 Jerome Dorris came from the family that owned the Dorris ranch just south of the Oregon border, and for which the town of Dorris is named. He was raised in the Christian Science belief that sees health as a function of mind. In his youth he was a cowboy, and trained horses. In the summer, he would ride the range for weeks at a time mending fences and rounding up stray cattle.

so that the Masters could give discourses through them. During the time from 1940 through 1949, except for a lapse during the Second World War, there were transmissions of about fifty discourses.[26]

In one of these discourses, Saint Germain spoke about marriage, no doubt to educate them about the changes in their relationship that were taking place.[27] He took a dim view of ordinary marriage, explaining what a limiting institution it could be when there was a feeling of ownership, that each partner possessed the other. There was also a feeling of limitation that occurred when partners thought they knew what was wrong with the other and held a fixed, often incorrect, perception of their partner—which drove that thought-form into their partner's consciousness. People, in fact, often perceived in their partner their own blind spot.

Pearl would soon see that the Masters had their own ideas about marriage, which did not always coincide with the conventional idea of two people staying married when the purpose of their association had finished. The Masters, who know everyone's karma, move people in and out of relationships, depending on what debts they have to each other, what lessons need to be learned, and what service they may have come together to perform. She saw how,

---

26 *Step by Step We Climb* (M. S. Princess, 1977).
27 *Step by Step We Climb to Freedom* (M. S. Princess, 1981). In the last book of the series, *Step by Step We Climb to Freedom and Victory* (M. S. Princess, 1983), Pearl speaks from the raised Christ Consciousness of her Higher Self.

when in service to the Masters, they often brought people together until their service was completed. For marriage to advance people spiritually, they needed to acknowledge the I AM Presence within each other and take responsibility for their own emotions, rather than blame each other for their own inadequacies.

Over the course of a few years, Pearl's Twin Ray, Bob, and his wife, Peggy, also divorced. Eventually Peggy married Pearl's former husband, Sydney. Then there was Loy, a former member of the Foundation who, on meeting Bob many years before, had heard inwardly, "This is the one you will marry," even though Bob was already married at that time. Now, finding themselves both single, Bob and Loy felt that they had been brought together by Saint Germain, and eventually married.

Pearl was happy to be single again, as she was a free spirit and not used to trying to live up to someone else's expectations. However, the Master had something else in store for her that was not anything she would have expected. After one of their meetings, Jerry was driving back to the ranch he was managing in Sonoma, when Saint Germain appeared before him in an etheric, yet visible form. Since he was not used to seeing things etherically, he knew that the Master had something important to say. He was shocked, however, when the Master said clearly, "I want you to marry Pearl."

The only contact he and Pearl had had prior to the formation of this group of former students at the ranch was when Pearl had sold him a copy of *Unveiled Mysteries* on his first visit to the I AM Sanctuary many years before. At one point he had seen a vision of himself holding

*Lady Master Pearl*

Pearl's hand as they walked up a golden staircase together, but had dismissed it as a daydream. When Pearl and her girlfriends in the Activity were in Golden Gate Park, they would often see Jerry ride by on his horse. They were on the beach one day when they saw the elusive cowboy riding toward them. Determined that he pay attention to them, they blocked his path, but Jerry, adhering to the rules about men and women not fraternizing, rode into the ocean and around them.

Now, at Saint Germain's appearance on the freeway, without a moment's hesitation, he made a U-turn and showed up back at Pearl's door. He knocked on the screen door. When Pearl answered, she asked, "So, what are you doing back here?"

"The Master wants us to get married," he blurted out, never one to mince words.

"What!" Pearl said, believing she had not heard correctly.

"Get your things, Pearl, the Master just told me to marry you."

"Look," Pearl said, emphatically, "Not only don't I love you, I don't even really like you that much."

"I know, Pearl, I feel the same way," Jerry said, apologetically. "None-the-less, it is the Master's wish. Don't worry; you can have your own room. I'll wait while you go and get your things."

In shock, Pearl told Jerry to wait in the kitchen. She went upstairs, sat down on the edge of her bed, and cried. She stared at the picture of Saint Germain on the wall. Looking into his eyes, she realized that it was true, that he truly did want her to marry Jerry. Slowly she gathered her few possession, threw them in a suitcase, and went downstairs.

They drove to the Sonoma courthouse in Santa Rosa, the place where the bear flag had first been raised in California, and in 1944, on the anniversary of that day, December 2nd, were married by the judge.

Managing the fruit ranch, they learned to work together. Pearl did the bookkeeping and cooking, which included preparing lunch for the ranch hands, while Jerry directed the work crews. They were close to Luther Burbank's farm, where Paramahansa Yogananda had come to visit the renowned botanist. Burbank had confessed to the great Indian yogi that he was able to achieve his miracles in plant breeding only by learning to love the plants.[28]

Pearl went there frequently, as she found it a restful place. The farm life gave her the grounding she needed after her years of intense spiritual work for the Masters. She was also trying to heal the inevitable scars from the dissolution of her marriage to Sydney, followed by the shock of her beloved Twin Ray marrying another woman. Even though she realized that these changes had happened under Saint Germain's direction, the emotional attachments were difficult to surrender. Although Jerry didn't speak much, he was kind, and tolerant of her often-impulsive nature. If she asked him to rearrange the furniture, he would comply willingly, and remain calm even when the next day she changed her mind and had him put everything back where it had been.

---

28 *Autobiography of a Yogi*, by Paramahansa Yogananda (Self-Realization Fellowship, 1946).

Jerry was, however, mystified by her claimed ability to be able to communicate with animals. While Jerry was working with a crew one day, far out in the fields, she heard Jerry's favorite horse, Modoc, say clearly to her, "I'm thirsty!"

She thought that was strange, as Jerry had installed an automatic water trough that normally refilled itself, but when Jerry came home she said, "Modoc is thirsty."

"That's not possible," he said, but to make Pearl happy he agreed to take a look. To his surprise, Pearl was right. The mechanism had jammed, and the water had run out.

When Jerry returned, he said, "How did you know there was a problem?"

"Modoc told me," she said again, as Jerry scratched his head, perplexed.

Again, a few months later she had a dream in which Modoc was speaking to her.

"The cows are in the vineyard," Modoc said.

"Wake up, Jerry, the cows are in the vineyard!"

"What? You're dreaming, Pearl, go back to sleep," he reassured her.

"No, Jerry, you've got to go check on the cows."

"What makes you think anything's wrong?" Jerry asked, as he began to wake.

"Modoc told me."

"Oh," he grunted, still doubtful, but he knew he wouldn't get back to sleep until he did as Pearl asked. He pulled on his boots and stumbled out into the dark. A half hour later he returned, "You were right, Pearl, the cows were in the vineyard."

After that Jerry paid more attention to her seemingly irrational requests, and accepted that his horse was in communication with his wife.

*Virginia Gildersleeve shaking hands with U.S. President Harry Truman, and with representatives of other countries, at the signing of the United Nations Charter in San Francisco, June 26th, 1945.*

# 16

## *Pearl and the United Nations*

In the midst of the Second World War, many nations signed a declaration of intent in 1942 to start an organization that would resolve future differences among nations. They were scheduled to vote on the Charter on June 25th, 1945, in San Francisco. Pearl was not a follower of politics, as she preferred to work on the Inner Planes to improve the world condition; however, one day she found herself almost thrust onto the world stage.

She was supposed to meet Jerry and a friend for lunch in Santa Rosa, but on the way she felt the unmistakable pull to drive instead toward San Francisco. Crossing the Golden Gate Bridge, and wondering where she was headed, she called to the Master Saint Germain. As she entered San Francisco, she continued on Lombard Street, affirming,

*I AM the presence of Saint Germain driving this car, taking me where I am meant to go.*

Soon she felt the pull to turn right, and proceeded down Van Ness Street. A few blocks from Market Street, she heard, "Park here." Still without knowing where she was supposed to go, she parked and started walking. In a few steps, a woman dressed formally came up to her and said, "Aren't you Pearl?"

"Why yes, I am, but how do you know me?"

*Lady Master Pearl*

"My dear, I attended one of the I AM classes that you taught, and your sincerity and innocence made such an impression, I could never forget you. My name is Virginia Gildersleeve, and I'm in town to help organize the meeting to approve the United Nations Charter.[29] In fact, I'm on my way there right now to meet President Truman. Why don't you come with me?"

Now Pearl realized that this must be the reason she had been guided here, and told Mrs. Gildersleeve she would be happy to go with her. Together, they walked the remaining blocks to the War Memorial Veterans Building. Inside was the largest group Pearl had ever seen. Mrs. Gildersleeve said that she had to go around back to meet the other delegates, but first she would make sure that Pearl got a good seat. Entering the auditorium of the Herbst Theater, Mrs. Gildersleeve escorted her down the aisle until they came to the front row. There in the center, amidst groups of officials from around the world, was one vacant seat. Climbing over a number of men, she reached it safely, and her escort departed.

As soon as the meeting started, Pearl felt a great spiritual radiation begin to permeate the atmosphere, which Pearl knew only the Ascended Masters could bestow—again, a confirmation that she was following the Masters' direction. Soon they would vote on the Charter, whose stated goal was to,

---

29 Virginia Gildersleeve (1877-1965) was a Dean of Barnard College, a crusader for women's rights, and the sole female delegate appointed to represent the United States at the U.N. Conference.

*Promote and encourage respect for human rights and fundamental freedoms for all, without distinction as to race, sex, language or religion.[30]*

Pearl called to the Masters, especially the Great Divine Director, to direct the proceedings and bring all into harmony with the Divine Plan. Then she called to her own mentor,

*Beloved Saint Germain, please come forth and take complete command here. Bring about the Perfect Divine Plan for the United Nations. Blaze the Violet Consuming Flame up, in, around, and through this auditorium, and dissolve and consume anything less than Perfection, by the Power of God that I AM.[31]*

Miraculously, they decided that instead of taking a formal vote, each representative from the fifty countries would instead stand and raise his or her hand if they wished to signal assent. It was a momentous occasion, about which the San Francisco Chronicle later said:

*The conference was not only one of the most important in history but, perhaps, the largest international gathering ever to take place.*

---

30 United Nations Charter.
31 The Violet Consuming Flame refers to the conscious invocation of the most purifying quality of the light spectrum, that of violet. It is not just an idea, but also a frequency of energy that, when invoked, can be felt and seen by those attuned to its activity. It burns up negative energy and raises whatever it touches into a more perfect state.

*Lady Master Pearl*

However, the document still needed to be signed, which was to take place the next day. Afterward, Mrs. Gildersleeve met Pearl on the street and said, "Dear, you must come back tomorrow. I will arrange it for you." Then she waved goodbye and disappeared in a cab with the American delegation.

When Pearl arrived home, she was concerned that Jerry might be upset because she had missed their lunch date, but he said that the friend they were expecting had canceled, so she hadn't missed a thing. After she told him where she had been, he said it was fine if she returned the next day, and that he would cook for the ranch hands.

The next day, the 26th of June, all the delegates and many foreign leaders gathered in the same auditorium to finally sign the United Nations Charter. True to her word, Mrs. Gildersleeve had arranged for Pearl to have her same seat. Along the back of the stage was a semi-circle of the flags of all the participating nations, and in the center was a huge round table. One by one the foreign leaders or their representatives came forward, sat at the table, and signed the document. Again, Pearl felt a tremendous energy that could only come from an Ascended Master activity.

Wondering where her friend was, whom she hadn't seen all day, suddenly she saw Mrs. Gildersleeve walk onstage. President Roosevelt had appointed her to the United States delegation shortly before his death, and now she sat to sign the document on behalf of the United States. After she was finished signing, President Truman stepped forward and warmly shook her hand. In his speech that followed he said,

*The Charter of the United Nations, which you have just signed, is a solid structure upon which we can build a better world.*

Pearl prayed that it would lead to a better world, but knew that it would take a lot more than signing a document to bring lasting peace to the world. She knew that the War was going on in the astral plane as well, and that those forces needed to be dissolved before humanity could be at peace.

As she drove home that evening she felt Saint Germain's presence, and that he was grateful to her for all her calls for the intercession of Ascended Masters. Even though the Masters are all-powerful, they generally do not interfere with human will. They require our invitation to intercede on our behalf.

*Lady Master Pearl*

## 17

## *Lady Master Leto's Reprimand*

Every New Year's Eve the Ascended Masters hold an inner retreat within the Royal Teton in the Teton Mountains of Wyoming. The Masters invite their students to attend to receive personal guidance and to participate in the Masters' outpouring of Light to the world. This year Pearl went to bed early in anticipation of the event, and prayed that she could go forth consciously, and remember on waking in the morning what had transpired. Soon she awakened in her finer body and found the beautiful Lady Master Leto standing beside her bed.[32]

"Beloved Pearl, in response to your sincere call, I have come to escort you to the Royal Teton," the Master said graciously. "Put this on," she said, handing Pearl a resplendent white gown that, as the fabric moved, gave off scintillating colors. Pearl had never seen anything like it, and in a moment she was regally attired to the envy of a princess.

Leto put her arm around Pearl's shoulder, and soon they were soaring into the night sky. Pearl could see the features of the landscape as they flew, until finally she saw

---

[32] Lady Master Leto helps people travel consciously out of the body. She had a past lifetime in Scotland in which she came to love the scent of heather, and she occasionally manifests that fragrance when she is present.

the peaks of the Tetons like spires in the distance. Soon they were descending an illumined passageway into the great council chamber of the Great White Brotherhood.

She was seated among the guests, some of whom she recognized from her group, and the service began. Some of the Masters with whom she was familiar were there, as well as many other Great Beings she had never seen, whose magnificence held her in awe. As they meditated together, a huge outpouring of Light went out to America. She knew that similar services were taking place in other retreats throughout the world, and that the Ascended Masters were imparting a new wave of consciousness to humanity that would move them toward the fulfillment of the Divine Plan.

After the close of the formal ceremony, the white-robed Saint Germain approached, his eyes seeming to look into her very soul, and with him was an individual whom Pearl sensed was someone she knew from past lives.

"I see that your intuition recognizes this old friend," Saint Germain said. "Although he has had many embodiments in India, you two have worked together in many past lifetimes back to the beginning of time. He has recently taken birth in the United States, and when the time is right, I will guide him to you for training. He will need that to present our Truth to the world. Now, dear Pearl, it is time for you to depart. Our sister who brought you here will escort you home."

Leto appeared by Pearl's side and, gently taking her hand, said, "Let us depart."

Again, they soared effortlessly through the night, Pearl in ecstasy at the Light that had been imparted to her. All too soon they were back in Santa Rosa, descending into her bedroom where her physical form lay sleeping. She hesitated to return to her dense form, which now seemed so limited and confining, but she thought, "If I could only keep this lovely robe, it would always remind me of this night."

"The robe," said Leto, obviously knowing Pearl's desire, but nevertheless, holding out her hand.

"Oh, but it's so beautiful; can't I keep it?"

"That is not permitted," Leto replied, firmly.

"Oh, but, I can't bear to part with it," Pearl insisted, clutching the scintillating folds of fabric to her bosom.

Leto stretched out her hand and, in a flash, snatched it away. In a stern voice, she said, "For this disobedience, you will not see me again for a very long time."

Then the exquisite, yet all-powerful Lady Master was gone, and Pearl was back in her physical form, asleep. In the morning, the subtle scent of heather filled the air, and she felt the exhilarating energy of the night's retreat permeating her body; but then the humiliating memory of her argument with Leto returned, and she was filled with shame. She wondered, wistfully, "How long will it be before I see Leto again?"

*Lady Master Pearl*

## 18

## *UFO Visitors*

Late one night Pearl was awakened by a humming sound, and walked out of her bedroom onto the balcony overlooking the orchards. There, in the field before the house, was a silvery metal disk, and a man and woman wearing jumpsuits walking toward the house. For some reason she felt no fear, and she waited as they climbed the stairs and walked toward her. They appeared to be normal humans, but exuded a sense of peace and self-mastery.

"We bring you a message," the man said, speaking quietly and gripping her upper arm tightly. After imparting his message, he concluded, "You will not remember what I have said until sometime in the future, when you will recall it as needed." He then released her arm and said, "Now, go back to bed."

As they turned and descended the stairs, Pearl went back inside. There, to her surprise, she saw her physical body on the bed. Perplexed for a minute, she said, "I AM taking command here, and getting back in my body," and the next thing she knew it was morning.

"Jerry, Jerry," Pearl said, "I had the most amazing visit last night."

"Must have been a dream," he said.

"No, it was real," Pearl affirmed, rubbing her arm that was still sore where the space traveler had gripped it. As if to reassure her that the visit had really occurred, the arm remained sore for several days. It was almost 30 years later that she gradually began to remember what she had been told, that these space people were our ancestors, who would be working closely with the Ascended Masters to help bring about the Divine Plan for humanity.

In March of 1954 a friend phoned Pearl with an invitation to visit George Adamski, whose book on UFOs had just been published.[33] He claimed to have actually been on board the crafts, and to generate publicity for the book was giving a talk at the Veterans Memorial Auditorium in Santa Rosa. At the end of the talk he called Pearl into another room, lit up a cigarette, and said, "You have something to tell me."

Unaware of what that might be, she turned her attention inward and thought, "I AM saying what I am meant to say."

As a message flashed on the screen of her mind, she said, "You are to stop fooling people and telling them that you are going up in the crafts."

"Yes, I know," he said, looking down sheepishly. "What else?"

Looking at the cigarette dangling from his lips, she was about to tell him to stop smoking. "I know, I know," he said, and took the cigarette out of his mouth and threw it on the floor. He ground it out on the cement with the heel of his shoe, then turned and walked away.

Years later, in 1975, Pearl would be visited a number

---

33 *Flying Saucers Have Landed,* by George Adamski and Desmond Leslie (British Book Center, 1953).

of times by Lt. Col. (Ret.) Wendelle Stevens, who had commanded the U. S. Air Force squadron that mapped the Arctic. His crews used to photograph numerous UFOs on the ice and coming up out of the ocean. He had just gone to Switzerland to investigate Eduard "Billy" Meier, the Swiss farmer who had been visited by a lady cosmonaut from the Pleiades by the name of Semjasse. Later, in 1989, while visiting Wendelle at his home in Tucson, he told me that he had seen Billy beamed up right in front of him as they walked out the kitchen door of Billy's home. Pearl believed that these visits were real, although when they stopped after about a year she was skeptical of the information Meier began to channel.[34] Gradually, Pearl developed sensitivity to these elder brothers and sisters from space, and would comment when she felt them working with people in the room.[35]

---

[34] Wendelle later told me in his home in Tucson, in 1989, that he had seen Billy beamed up right in front of him as Billy walked out the kitchen door. He had just told him that he was about to have a contact.

[35] Wendelle Stevens (1923-2010), author of *UFO Contact from the Pleiades: A Preliminary Investigative Report,* with Lee Elders (Genesis III, 1980), and first Director of Investigations for the Aerial Phenomena Research Organization (APRO) in Tucson, Arizona.

*Fence posts that Pearl and Jerry installed on their ranch in Edgewood.*

## 19

## *Mount Shasta Calls*

Clad in the whiteness of her seven glaciers, Mount Shasta stood out boldly on the horizon. Ever since Pearl had read of Godfre Ray King's meeting with Saint Germain on its slopes in *Unveiled Mysteries,* she had felt drawn to the Mountain. On vacation in 1956, Pearl and Jerry drove through the rugged town of Dorris, where he had been raised. Only sixty miles away, the Mountain seemed to be pulling them like a magnet. Later that day they arrived in the town of Mount Shasta, then only a small mill town at the Mountain's base.

Simultaneously they looked at each other and realized they had both had the same idea, of relocating to the Mountain. They called a real estate agent to see what was available. They knew that if they were meant to move, it would happen easily, a sign that it was a Master Plan, and not merely a passing whim.

Despite the persistence of the real estate agent, they didn't feel attracted to any of the houses he showed; yet, seemingly by accident, they kept arriving back at a small cottage under some towering evergreen trees. It wasn't on the market, but when the agent called the owner, he discovered they wanted to sell. Pearl and Jerry recognized now that circumstances were aligning with their inner feelings, a sure sign of Guidance—so they made a low offer, which was immediately accepted.[36] Almost effortlessly, they

---

36 Pearl frequently said that the only way to separate true

*Lady Master Pearl*

found themselves moving to the town that was legendary among mystic seekers.[37]

They had enough money left over from the sale of the ranch in Santa Rosa to also buy a small ranch in nearby Edgewood. They rented out their new home and moved to the ranch. Once again Pearl found herself canning fruits and vegetables in a steaming kitchen, cooking lunch for farmhands, and helping Jerry dig postholes for fences in the hard, lava-encrusted earth. They had to char the posts in a fire in a 55-gallon drum so that insects wouldn't bore into them. Today, the fences they worked so hard to erect are still in use. (See preceding photo.)

A few years later they moved again, this time east of the Mountain to the town of Burney, where Jerry was hired to manage another ranch. While there they took a correspondence course in motel management. Although they passed the course, they still lacked any practical experience. One day as they were driving along, they came to a small motel and decided to make the owners an offer. They would manage the motel for free for the weekend just for the experience. As the owners hadn't had

---

    guidance from the many false voices is to follow the feeling in one's heart.

37  Mount Shasta, known around the world as one of the seven great mystic mountains, has been visited by renowned spiritual teachers such as: Madame H. P. Blavatsky, Meher Baba, Swami Vivekananda, Mata Amritanandamayi, and many venerable Tibetan Lamas.

a vacation since they had bought the place almost twenty years before, they were overjoyed—and the couple was soon out the door.

Toward the end of the day, Pearl noticed that if she blessed a car as it passed, many times it would stop and come back, and the people would rent a room. This continued for several hours until the motel was full, and she hung out the No Vacancy sign.

When the owners returned on Sunday, they were shocked, for in all their years running the motel they had never rented every unit.

"What on Earth did you do?" the woman asked.

"Oh, I just sent love to people," Pearl replied.

Eventually, the owners of the ranch in Burney said they didn't need Jerry any more as they were returning to run it themselves, and Pearl and Jerry moved back to their home in Mount Shasta. They still needed to earn a living, so, presenting the excellent letter of recommendation from the motel they had managed, they got a job as a couple, managing the Mountain Air Motel (now the Shasta Inn) on South Mount Shasta Boulevard. When Pearl's spiritual work started, Jerry got a job at the Shasta Royal Motel near Dunsmuir. When it was bought by the Saint Germain Foundation and converted into an I AM Sanctuary, he got a job back in Mount Shasta, at the Tree House Motel. This freed Pearl from having to help earn a living, so that she would be ready for the students the Masters would soon send.

*Lady Master Pearl*

*Several rock bands at the home of the Grateful Dead, 710 Ashbury St., San Francisco, 1967.*

# 20

## *Haight-Ashbury*

After the spiritual acceleration Pearl received during her service to the Ascended Masters with Godfre Ray King, she and Jerry returned to what appeared to be a normal life in the 1950s. Although they had achieved a deep inner wisdom, the western culture was oriented to the pursuit of the Eight Worldly Dharmas: attachment to pleasure, avoidance of pain; pursuit of fame, and the avoidance of anonymity; pursuit of praise, and the avoidance of blame; and the pursuit of gain, and the avoidance of loss—polarities which guaranteed continual re-embodiment on Earth over and over again.

These goals were more understandable for the previous generation that had grown up during the Great Depression, where many had to struggle for survival, and counted themselves fortunate if they had a place to sleep and three meals a day. Then there was the Second World War. When the men returned home after the war, it was not the same world. Women had proved their independence, and the old ways of relating no longer worked. People did not know how to communicate, and instead repressed their feelings. The kids could feel the suffering of their parents, and longed for an escape.[38]

---

38 John Welwood coined the term "spiritual bypassing" to describe this tendency to use spirituality to avoid facing unresolved emotional issues. See his

*Lady Master Pearl*

That promise of freedom came in the 60s in the form of drugs, sex, and rock 'n' roll. It was the time to *do your own thing*, and people like Timothy Leary were saying, "Turn on, tune in, and drop out." Unfortunately, without any guidance from enlightened beings, many simply turned on with drugs and dropped out, without ever tuning in. Kids left or were kicked out of their homes, joined communes, or went on the road in search of truth through experience. Many gathered in San Francisco, specifically the Haight-Ashbury district, which became a haven for the counter-culture. Rock groups like The Mamas and the Papas made the area even more famous with songs like "California Dreamin'."

It was into this scene that, one day in 1969, Pearl and Jerry descended, seemingly by accident. While trying to take a shortcut through San Francisco, they found themselves on Haight Street, trapped by a crowd of hippies headed to a rock concert in Golden Gate Park. A bearded, barefoot man smoking marijuana pounded on the hood of the car. Jerry froze, but the man smiled and shouted, "Hey man, loosen up!"

"Roll up your window," Jerry shouted to Pearl, "These people look dangerous."

A girl in an old-fashioned dress and beaded headband

---

book, *Toward a Psychology of Awakening: Buddhism, Psychotherapy and the Path of Personal and Spiritual Transformation* (Shambhala, 2002). See also, *Spiritual Bypassing: When Spirituality Disconnects Us from What Really Matters,* by Robert Augustus Masters (North Atlantic Books, 2010).

came up to Pearl, leaned in the window, and handed her a flower.

"I love you," she said, her large, brown eyes looking into Pearl's.

"Why thank you," Pearl said, and smiled back, deeply touched.

Watching the procession go by, Pearl heard her Inner Presence say, "These are your people." Pondering on what that might mean, she remembered that once Saint Germain had said, "In the future, young people will come to you with large, wide-open eyes, and they will awaken spiritually as if overnight."

"Are these those people?" Pearl wondered.

The rock group Crosby, Stills and Nash was performing in San Francisco that summer, and lead guitarist David Crosby's brother, Ethan, would soon move to Mount Shasta—and be one of the first of this new generation to sit in Pearl's living room.

*Lady Master Pearl*

## 21

## *Two Sent by the Masters*

Pearl and Jerry lived quiet lives, keeping to themselves and not telling anyone about their past activity in the Saint Germain Foundation. Although Mrs. Ballard had created a major branch of the Saint Germain Foundation in Mount Shasta, their members were often viewed with some suspicion by the locals, due to their strange dress code and the arrogance with which they looked down on non-members.

In the 1800s, nine different Native American peoples lived within sight of the Mountain. Around 1820, many white settlers came to the area, which rapidly became inhabited by miners, loggers, mill hands, and the Italian families who established fruit orchards in the valley. Famous for its strawberries, it had at one time been called Strawberry Valley, then Berryvale, and Sisson. In 1905 it was finally incorporated as the Town of Mount Shasta, then in 1925, the City of Mount Shasta.

Pearl's work began on her birthday, October 20th, 1972, with the arrival of two young seekers, Jim and Telos.[39] They had arrived at the Golden Mean Metaphysical

---

39  Telos had taken the name of a mystical city supposedly located in the Four Corners area of the American Southwest, as claimed by George Hunt Williamson, author of *Secret Places of the Lion* (Neville Spearman, 1958). A psychic using the name Sharula, a character

Bookstore in Ashland, Oregon, about 60 miles north, and had asked about the Ascended Masters. The owner, Maxine McMullen, sent them to Mount Shasta, giving them the phone number of Fran Lewis, who she thought might be able to give them some guidance.[40] When they reached town, Fran told them to come over, for she was having a birthday party for her friend, Pearl.

Although Pearl didn't like parties, Fran had been one of her early supporters, and she felt that she ought to attend. Only a half dozen people were there, but when she met Jim and Telos she was startled, as she recognized their faces from a recent dream. She kept the dream to herself, but left the party as soon as she was politely able. Hardly had she arrived home, when there was a knock at the door. Opening it, there stood Jim and Telos.

"Well, this is a surprise! What brings you here?" Pearl asked. "And how do you know where I live?"

"We followed you," they said, embarrassed. "We want to know about the Ascended Masters, and when we felt your energy, we knew that you must be in contact with them. Please tell us what you know."

---

    she read about in a novel, later relocated this city to Mount Shasta. See *Mount Shasta Myths Exploded: Adama, Sananda and the Recent City of Telos* by Juan Hunu (www.Smashwords.com, 2012).

40  Ibid. Fran Lewis, Sister Thedra, and Sister Wali had all been disciples of one of the first New Age gurus in Los Angeles, Krishna Venta, as referenced in the previous book by Juan Hunu. After his demise in 1958, these three women moved to Mount Shasta and began channeling their former teacher, still believing he was the Christ.

Pearl hesitantly invited them in, but said, "I can't spend too much time with you, as my 'Hubby' is at work, and will be home soon."

She told them a little about the Masters, especially Saint Germain, and his teaching of the I AM. She helped them still their minds, turn their attention inward, and contact their own I AM Presence. Moved profoundly by the Light they felt, they thanked Pearl and started to leave. Hesitating in the doorway, they asked, "Can we come back again sometime?"

"Yes, sometime," she said, not dreaming that they would be back the following weekend, this time with an entire carload of friends, and that on her 67th birthday her true work had just commenced.

*L. to R: Mary Carol Doane, Pearl Dorris, Bill Gaum, Debbie Kaemmerer, and Author, circa 1985.*

## 22

## *I Meet Pearl*

At the end of the road, her house appeared to be something from a fairy tale, surrounded by a tall hedge, sheltered beneath a grove of pine trees. I walked through the rose covered trellis with a sense of apprehension, as though entering a temple from which I would emerge, forever transformed. At the end of the flagstone pathway, I came to a heavy oak door, rounded at the top, and stood before it, hesitating, before I let the iron knocker fall with a decisive thud.[41]

The door was opened by a gentle-faced woman in her sixties, but with piercing, hazel eyes that were as unflinching and penetrating as those of an owl, and she said, "Come in, I've been expecting you."

"Expecting me?" I replied, already feeling ordinary reality disappearing, as she escorted me into the cozy living room and pointed out a chair opposite hers.

"The Master Saint Germain came to me this morning and said that he was sending someone to see me," she said, as though used to daily visits from the Masters who guided the destiny of humanity.

"He did?" I gulped, wondering if perhaps he was in a

---

41 This chapter is partially excerpted from my autobiography, *Adventures of a Western Mystic, Part I: Apprentice to the Masters,* Chapter 3, by Peter Mt. Shasta (Church of the Seven Rays, 2010).

back room and might enter at any moment. Pearl beckoned me closer.

"I have been waiting for you."

I looked at the *Reader's Digest* on the table beside her, and at the tapestry on the wall of a deer wandering through a forest, and wondered, "After all my wanderings in India, sitting at the feet of nearly naked gurus with dreadlocks, who smeared their faces with ash and colored paste, has God really brought me to this remote town to receive spiritual teachings from a grandmotherly housewife?"

"So, who did you visit in India?" Pearl asked.

"Over the past two years I visited a lot of different saints and sages," I explained, "Neem Karoli Baba, Anandamayi Ma, Shivabala Yogi, and many others; but most recently Sathya Sai Baba."

When I mentioned Sai Baba, her face lit up and she exclaimed, "Oh, he is beautiful!"

"You can feel him?" I asked.

"Don't you feel him? He's right here in the room."

Suddenly, as I turned my attention inward, I did feel him, and suddenly felt close to tears. I had not felt his overwhelming love since I had sat at his feet two months before.

"How did you do that?" I asked.

"Do what?"

"How did you bring him here?

"I just sent love to him the same way I would send love to an Ascended Master, and he responded. That is the Law of their Being. When you send love to them, they are drawn to you. I said, 'Sai Baba, I love you and want to know more about you,' and he responded."

Receiving the darshan of Sai Baba flooding us with waves of love, we sat there in bliss. Then, suddenly Pearl looked up at me and asked, "Now, who is that?"

"Who do you mean?"

"There is another Master here now, also from India. He has a turban and is standing beside you. I am asking who he is."

She fell silent, looking at the floor for a moment, then looked up. "Does the name Vivekananda mean anything to you?"

"Why yes, he was the first Indian yogi to introduce yoga to America, and my first spiritual inspiration."

"Now, there is another great one," Pearl said, nodding to my other side. "This one I saw once before, on the day he left his body. His name is Sri Aurobindo."

Pearl sat motionless, her attention turned inward and eyes looking down at the floor, and then said, "There is some great reason these beings have come here with you today. They are showing me that it is because you are to continue their work of bringing the East and West together. I have never experienced anything like this before."

We sat in silence, feeling the blessings of these three great souls from India, and then Pearl said, "Would you like to meditate?"

"Sure," I said, starting to slide onto the floor to fold my legs in lotus posture as I had been taught.

"You don't need to sit on the floor to meditate," Pearl said, smiling.

"Really?"

"Yes, you can meditate just fine sitting in a chair."

"OK, I'll try," I said, feeling that I was abandoning the

yogic tradition of austerity, by sitting upright in the chair. As I shut my eyes, Pearl uttered another instruction that shocked me yet again, "You don't need to close your eyes to meditate either."

"What! This is too much," I thought. "This is because westerners are just lazy. How can you meditate sitting in a chair with your eyes open?" Although her words contradicted everything I had been taught, I decided to comply, and let my gaze fall on a spot on the floor.

"Eyes up," she corrected. "We are going to meditate with our eyes open, looking at each other. The open gaze completes the circuit. Now, turn your attention inward and feel the center of your being. Feel the great Light within that is the Source of your Being."

Doing as she requested, I felt a quickening in the center of my chest. As I looked toward her, she seemed to emanate energy from her heart to mine.

"Now, say silently to yourself, 'I AM the Living Light,' and visualize a sun within you."

I did as she asked, turning my attention deeper and deeper within, and all the while continuing to gaze at her, and when I said, "I AM the Living Light," a light flashed into the room.

"That's it!" I shouted in amazement.

"That's what?" she asked.

"The Light! I have finally seen the Light that I have read about and that everyone talks about. I have seen it inwardly, but have never seen it come out before. This is what I have been looking for. This is what I have been traveling all over the world to find, and now here it is."

"You have just given me my answer," Pearl said.

"What answer?"

"People have been telling me that my way is too simple, that I should give it up and follow the eastern path. I have been asking Saint Germain if I should do that, and he told me this morning, 'Today you will have your answer.' You have given me the answer he promised."

*Pearl and Jerry's former home in Mount Shasta, 2014.*

## 23

## *We Invoke Saint Germain*

"So, how did you find me today?" Pearl asked.

I told her of my experience in Muir Woods—the encounter with the mysterious stranger who had materialized out of thin air and taken me out of my body to an etheric realm. He would have allowed me to remain if I wished, but when I saw the pain of humanity, it seemed there was no choice but to return and help. After accompanying me back to Muir Woods, my escort, who by now I realized was no ordinary being, then transformed before my eyes into a Master in a white robe. He told me that I had made the right choice, and that now we would be working closely together. His parting words were, "Go to Mount Shasta. The first person you meet there will tell you what to do next." That person was Stephen at the health food store, and he told me, "You need to meet Pearl."[42]

Without showing any surprise, and with a mischievous twinkle in her eye, Pearl asked, "And who do you suppose that stranger was in Muir Woods?"

I nodded toward the picture of Saint Germain I saw on her wall.

"He is here now, and he is indicating that he wants to help you," she said.

"What is he saying?" I asked, astonished that suddenly, out of the blue, this Master was showing so much interest

---

42   Ibid.

in me. I wondered, "Where has he been all my life, during all my ordeals? Why did he wait until now to appear? Where was he in the past when I prayed to God, and no one answered?"

"I can't tell you what he is saying because I am not allowed to channel the words of the Masters," Pearl responded. "The Masters do not allow their students to channel, except on the rarest occasions, because the Masters—who are God beings—can convey their wishes *directly* to you through your own mind and feelings. You may not hear the words they are saying—for your mind would only argue with them and interfere. Instead, they convey information to your Higher Mental Body, which you later access spontaneously as intuition."

I remembered now with embarrassment how I had argued with Saint Germain on the Mountain the year before, not knowing who he was. He had come in his more etheric form and spoken directly to my mind, telling me to change my name, as well as many other things that I did not want to do. No wonder the Masters hesitate to tell people the future, because it is frequently not the future they desire. Now Pearl was saying how I could contact Saint Germain within myself and merge with his consciousness.

"Go within and turn your attention to the center of your being, and send love to Saint Germain—affirming his presence within yourself, knowing that his heart and your heart are one—you will feel his presence. That will open the way for him to work directly with you through your heart."

I shut my eyes, but Pearl ordered once again, "Open

eyes! Turn your attention within to the center of your being, and say silently within yourself, 'I AM the presence of Saint Germain!'

"Feel the sun within your heart, and within that sun feel his presence. You are not claiming to be the Master, but learning to recognize the oneness of the Master's consciousness with yours.

"The Masters are not separate from you," Pearl continued. "There is no distance or time for them—wherever you are, they are also. Oneness with Saint Germain is possible because the energy of the Seventh Ray, of which Saint Germain is Chohan (head), is within you. That energy is part of you, like part of your own inner rainbow that you are invoking, the part of yourself to which the Master corresponds.

"Just as daylight is composed of all seven colors of the spectrum, so too are you composed of all seven rays of creation. There is an Ascended Master who is the Chohan of each ray, though now we are invoking only the Seventh Ray.[43]

"He is watching you, and you should call on him if you want his help, if you want to invoke him into your life. This is the same way you would invoke Jesus. To contact Saint Germain, you need only go within and open your heart. These two are brothers, working together. The Master sees you not as separate, but as a part of himself, and so you

---

43 The Seventh Ray is that of the incoming Aquarian Age. For more information on the Rays, see *The Rays and the Initiations*, by Alice A. Bailey (Lucis Trust, 1960).

should see him and not hesitate to call upon him. When you say, 'I AM here, I AM there, I AM everywhere,' you touch on his consciousness—the awareness that within the One is the many, and within the many is the One."

I did as Pearl instructed, repeating over and over to myself,

*I AM the Presence of Saint Germain.*

At first I felt nothing, only embarrassing silence. Then I began to feel a stream of happiness, accompanied by an electrifying presence. The atmosphere of the room seemed charged with violet light. Pearl acknowledged the sudden, violet tinge to the atmosphere, and said, "*That* is the Master Saint Germain—and he is very happy. He has verve—a word that combines vitality and nerve. Verve means let's get with it—but with a sense of humor."

I had thought that the Masters were always serious, but now I could swear that Saint Germain was laughing, and I was having a hard time holding back my own laughter.

"Do the Masters laugh, Pearl?"

"Yes, Saint Germain has a great sense of humor. In fact, he is laughing now."

I finally let go of my own laughter, and when I was relaxed a stream of energy poured down through the crown of my head and into the center of my chest, filling my body with light. I heard, within the center of my being, the resounding affirmation over and over,

*"I AM THAT I AM…I AM THAT I AM…*
*I AM THAT I AM."*

As the consciousness of the Source became anchored

in my heart, the violet hue of the room intensified. I continued to look into Pearl's eyes, amazed, as her physical form seemed to dissolve into a luminous ball of golden light. In that timeless awareness there was no past or future, only now, and we both basked in the light of that Inner Sun.

As the light faded, gradually I became aware of my body and of Pearl sitting across from me. It was hard to believe that this transformation had happened, not at the feet of a yogi in India, but sitting in a chair in the living room of this elderly lady. I looked again at the deer grazing in the tapestry on the wall and the wooden elves staring at me mischievously from their perches on the bookshelves. Then, Pearl continued as though she were seeing the contents of my mind.

"Even though you heard no words of direction, you have been given guidance, encouragement, and nourishment, which the Master has imparted to your Higher Mental Body, and as the occasion calls it forth, you will be able to access this information. For me to channel a message would only weaken you by causing you to look outside yourself. The Masters want you to go within for your answers, and in that way you will become a Master, rather than a perpetual follower of the Masters.

"On rare occasions the Masters have given spiritual discourses through highly developed individuals who have been well-prepared over many years, such as my mentor, Godfre Ray King. However, at those times, the Masters were giving spiritual law and imparting a radiation that strengthened the self-awareness of the individuals present, not prophecies that fill people with fear, or that keep them coming back for ever more information and high sounding initiations that make them feel superior.[44]

"All contact with a true Master takes a person closer to the Source within, leaving one feeling empowered. Only false prophets try to turn attention to themselves, or barrage their followers with a never-ending stream of information and prophesies, which for the most part are rubbish.

"As for charging money to hear a Master speak," Pearl went on, "No one who has ever been so blessed as to stand in the presence of a Master would ever consider charging someone money for that same privilege, assuming the privilege was even his or hers to dispense. When people are excluded from a Master for financial reasons, you know there is no Master, at least not a spiritual Master. I am not talking about charging to cover expenses, or requesting donations.

"Many sincere 'channels' think they are hearing the Masters, but most are merely hearing their own minds, or they are contacting disembodied spirits masquerading as Masters, that drift about sucking the energy of their followers. Even though the information these channelers

---

[44] One of the major causes of dissention in the Theosophical Society, as well as many other spiritual groups, is the thinly veiled ego drive to advance beyond one's peers in the supposed attainment of ever-greater blessings and initiations. The beauty of Pearl's teaching, like that of Jesus, is its utter simplicity, that the Kingdom of God within you is present at every moment.

give may sometimes be accurate or inspiring, it may also be untrue—and give rise to fear, false expectations, and harmful actions. These earthbound entities know they will catch more flies with honey than with vinegar, so they often lace misleading information with accurate observations and flattering comments that appeal to the ego, telling you how great you have been in past lives, or how great you will be in the future.

"The highest form of guidance manifests as spontaneous action, free from thought. It flows intuitively from the center of your being, without any need for interpretation. You simply *do what is right!* You know what you need, when you need it, and you act in the moment from your Higher Self, with no intermediary."

Pearl paused, and then continued her explanation of how the Masters work. "The Masters guide and direct without people even knowing most of the time, allowing the guidance to be perceived as intuition or even desire. You only become a Master by learning to tune into your own Higher Self, the *I AM THAT I AM,* not by getting information from someone else. How do you think these beings became Masters?" she asked. "By becoming conscious of their Higher Selves, the same process by which you too, will become a Master. There is no other way, and it is not the work of a day.

"People read a book, attend a seminar, or have a channeling, and they think they are Masters and want to give workshops. It takes time and effort to overcome the lower nature, and strict obedience to the Higher Self and the Masters. Saint Germain said one day, 'If any individual will give total obedience, I can help even a shoe shine boy

*Lady Master Pearl*

in the train station clear his karma and achieve liberation in three years.'"

I straightened up at this news, which I took as an offer from Saint Germain. Pearl glanced over with a knowing smile, "But let me caution you. Once you embark on this path, you will be severely tested—of that you may be sure. You must walk the razor's edge. Woe to the student who, having embarked on this path, turns back, for *there is no turning back.*"

Pearl finished, and I sat still in my chair, feeling the great power in the silence. Now, I knew why I had been brought here. My whole life had led to this moment. Saint Germain had made an offer, to open the door to the Great Work of self-mastery. It is a paradoxical path, for to become a Master you do not dwell on the Masters, but on your own Eternal Self. The Masters assist in the process, but the real work is within.

The words she spoke resonated so deeply with me that I vowed to make whatever sacrifice was necessary, to discipline myself in whatever way was needed—little dreaming how difficult this would often be. I requested Saint Germain, whose presence still filled the room, to take me as his apprentice—and I knew that he heard my vow. I did not realize, though, how soon the lessons would begin, and how severe the tests were to be over the next several years. At that moment, sitting in Pearl's living room, I felt only elation that after so many years of searching, I had at last found the being who would lead me on that sacred quest.

It had become dark outside. Our meeting had lasted hours. Now feeling that our time was at an end, I asked the question that had been on my mind since she opened the door. "Pearl, when I came in, why did you say that you had been waiting for me?"

Her answer was an astonishing one. "Many years ago I was taken on New Year's Eve to the retreat in the Royal Teton. Saint Germain introduced you to me and said that in the future he would bring us together—that I was to prepare you for your work with him.

"That night I committed a great blunder for which I was severely reprimanded," she continued, "Now, after almost thirty years, I have finally been forgiven. I was visited last night by the one toward whom I was disobedient, and she told me that your arrival was imminent."

"And who was that?" I asked.

"Lady Master Leto."

*Lady Master Pearl*

*Pearl in her garden, circa 1975.*

## 24

## *The Magic Switchboard*

I felt that I had gotten Pearl's message, which was a simple one after all the elaborate tantric visualizations I had learned in India: *Meditate on the Light within. Hold the vision you want to manifest, and use the words "I AM" to bring your vision into being.* What more is there? I was not a groupie to sit at a teacher's feet, so had no plans to return to see her.

Yet, one day as I was driving around town I had the unmistakable feeling to go see Pearl again. I resisted, but finally the feeling got so strong that I pulled into the Safeway parking lot (now Rite Aid), turned off the engine, and sat there to still my mind. But, there was no point in meditating, for all I could think of was Pearl. I kept seeing her face before me, and the longer I sat there the more insistent her expression became. Finally, I noticed a pay phone booth at the other end of the parking lot. I walked over, dropped a coin in the slot, and dialed her number. She answered immediately, "Where have you been? You were supposed to be here an hour ago!"

"Oh, I didn't realize that I could come back again," I stammered apologetically.

"You have kept the Master waiting," she said, "Get up here immediately."

It's a small town, so I was at her door in a few minutes. To my surprise, there were a dozen other cars parked along the sides of the street that ended in front of her house.

*Lady Master Pearl*

Inside, I found that all her other students were gathered there in a circle. I sat down quietly, hoping that she would not scold me again.

"Now that everyone is here, we can begin," she said. "The Masters have shown me that there is grave danger of an earthquake in China, and they want us to send our energy there. Turn your attention inward to your God Flame in the center of your being, and feel that great Christ Light. Now say,

*I AM the Sun of God.*

"Feel that Light surging within you, and let it expand outward. Imagine you are translucent as crystal, and feel its rays illuminating your being and world. You are now a great Sun, one with the Great Central Sun, and you say silently within yourself, 'I AM sending my Light to China, stabilizing the earth there, by the Power of God that I AM.' We offer this energy to the Ascended Masters to amplify and direct as needed."

As we sat there, immersed in the field of Light we had created, I felt everything shimmering, as though dissolving. Everything and everyone was bathed in Light. After a while Pearl called our attention back into the human dimension and said that the Masters had been able to lessen the earthquake that would otherwise have caused great damage and loss of life, and that they were expressing their gratitude.

"Next time," Pearl said, looking directly at me, "When you feel the urge to do something, and it does not leave, no matter how hard you try to eliminate it, follow through on your feeling—for it is through your feelings that God guides you."

As I left her house, I asked others if Pearl had phoned them?

"No, we just felt that inner pull, and came up. When we saw everyone else arriving, we knew we had received the Inner Call. Once you're tuned in, the Masters can call you on the Cosmic Switchboard."

After that, I paid closer attention to those subtle feelings which, when obeyed, lead to right action. I came to see that *a large part of Mastery is not in exerting your personal will, but in surrendering to Divine Will.* When you are in that flow, you lead a life of synchronicity, finding yourself always at the right place at the right time. Once you have perceived the Plan, then your own energy, whose source is God, is invoked.

I saw that Divine Switchboard in action many times during the next few years. As many as thirty people would come from all over town and show up at Pearl's door within minutes of each other.

On another of these occasions, when the Masters again asked us to direct energy to avert an earthquake, the meeting lasted into the night. The energy became overwhelming and Pearl said that the Masters wanted us to remain together throughout the night, leaving our bodies consciously to continue our work together. In any case, people could hardly walk, let alone drive. I always carried a sleeping bag and mat in my van, as by now I was used to being sent on missions that took me to almost inaccessible places, where there was no place to sleep other than the back of my van—so I slept outside with my head against Pearl's wall. She sent Jerry up into the attic, where there was a cot, and turned his bedroom into a girl's dormitory

*Lady Master Pearl*

for the night. The other guys slept on the sofa or the living room floor, wrapped in the blankets Pearl handed out.

In the morning, when we all gathered in her living room, bleary-eyed, Pearl said, "You are becoming part of the Great White Brotherhood. It starts out by learning to be obedient in small things like this, but gradually you are trusted with greater assignments. The Ascended Masters are also moving upward in their evolution, and some day you will fill their positions. Your everyday life is your training school for this Mastery."

*Pearl and Jerry at home in Mount Shasta (Photo by Leila).*

# 25

## *Challenges*

As the number of seekers arriving to visit Pearl grew, her challenges also increased. Not everyone who came to see her was able to understand the simple beauty of her teachings, or to assimilate the intense energy that the Masters poured forth in her presence. Some were unbalanced psychologically, and had unresolved personal issues to work out, which they projected onto Pearl. One of these people was a young man named Thomas who, like the disciple of Jesus by the same name, doubted everything. Pearl asked me to talk with him and see if I could get him more into his heart. When I did as she asked, he flew into a rage.

At Pearl's home one evening, he interrupted Pearl with a question. No one ever did this, because people were usually raised to such a level of consciousness that there was nothing to ask. Thomas' question, however, was not a desire to know the truth, but a statement that contained the hidden barb of hostility.

Pearl rose to her feet and, with a power I had never seen, pointed to the door and said, "Get out!"

Everyone was shocked. No one had seen this wrathful side of the usually serene Divine Mother. "I said 'get out,'" she repeated.

Thomas rose to his feet, climbed over everyone's knees in the packed room, and stumbled out. Next day Pearl asked me to speak to him, and to tell him not to come back again. Many thought she had been too harsh, but Pearl saw a force within Thomas that would soon reveal its destructive nature.

Meanwhile, there was another threat directed at Pearl, this time from the Saint Germain Foundation. One of their members, Guy Kerr, would park his car outside Pearl's house every day and write down a record of everyone going in and out, which today would probably be called "stalking." Perhaps they were jealous of all the young people attracted to Pearl, as few young people were now joining their organization. After Godfre's transition, many other individuals and groups began disseminating the same or similar information. In order to prevent that, Mrs. Ballard had gone so far as to file trademark registration of key expressions of Saint Germain's work for humanity, such as "Violet Flame" and the "I AM Teachings," and Pearl felt the Foundation resented her giving these teachings as an individual.[45]

Soon both these threats would neutralize each other in a most dramatic way, with the unfolding of a

---

[45] Even though the Saint Germain Foundation filed trademark registration on the expression, "Violet Consuming Flame," it is described freely on their website, which goes on to say that these teachings come from the Masters and should be given to freely to humanity. The website says "...the actual focusing, projecting, and sustaining of the Violet Consuming Flame is done by (the individual's) own 'Beloved Mighty I AM Presence,' for It is God's Flame of Pure Divine Love." If, as they say, it is an activity of God, it cannot be owned or its use curtailed by any group.

deadly mutual karma. Guy allowed Thomas to camp on his land, and one day they got into a metaphysical argument. In a rage, Thomas shot and killed him and was sentenced to prison.

One day a group of students of a Tibetan Lama, Tarthang Tulku, moved to town. A few of them came to sit with Pearl one evening, but they seemed surrounded in a cloud of skepticism. It seemed they had not come to learn anything, but to scout out what Pearl was doing that attracted so many students. The next day the head of the group, Durga, came to see Pearl and announced, "We are going to begin giving our Vajrayanna teachings, which are far more advanced than what you are teaching. I just wanted to explain to you that we will be taking your students,"

"They are not my students," Pearl explained, unconcerned. "You are welcome to them if they get more out of what you are teaching than what is going on here. It's fine with me."

Attendance dropped at Pearl's group for about a month; then people began coming back. In another month, attendance at Durga's group had dropped to almost nothing, and by spring most of the group had left town. Durga, however, remained. She was pregnant, and even though her boyfriend had left to join another Buddhist group to the north, she wanted to have the baby in Mount Shasta.

One day the phone rang, and when Pearl answered she was surprised to hear Durga's worried voice, "Pearl, please, please help me. My baby is due, but his head won't turn down. I don't want a Cesarean, and I don't know what to do. Please help me."

"Just a minute," Pearl said, and put the phone down. Silently, she said, "I AM the Presence of God come forth now, taking complete command of Durga's baby, and turning its head down right this moment!"

When she picked up the phone again, Durga said, "Oh, it's moving! I can feel something happening," and as they continued to talk Durga described how the baby's head was moving toward the birth canal. The baby was born the next day, and a few days later Durga came to see Pearl. She placed the baby in Pearl's arms and said, "Pearl, please forgive me for what I did. I'm so sorry. You are a saint. Please bless my little girl."

There were many stories in town about Pearl. One day I ran into a friend, Bill, who had been to see Pearl with a group of eight other people. After they left they compared notes on what had happened, but they could not agree. Each had heard something different, yet each one's questions were answered. He went on to say that he used to dress up as a clown for various festivities. He hadn't seen Pearl in a few years, but one day he was downtown in his clown outfit, his face completely hidden, and Pearl had walked up to him and said, "Hi Bill, how are you doing?" She had seen right through his costume.[46]

Pearl was the subject of a lot of gossip as well as outright hostility from her neighbors and other townspeople, who

---

46  Story told to me by Bill Buffalo on November 6, 2014.

did not understand what she was doing. Seeing all the young men showing up at her door while Jerry was at work, some neighbors claimed she was having affairs. Even when they admitted to her they knew she was faithful to her husband, they envied her popularity and complained to her about the influx of hippies into the neighborhood.

In 1973, Mount Shasta was a logging town, and many locals regarded even tourists with suspicion, and kids with backpacks and long hair with actual hostility. Signs on the doors of businesses on Mount Shasta Boulevard read, "No Hippies Allowed."[47] Yet, an increasing number of young people continued to move into town to study with Pearl. After leaving her home in a state of God intoxication, some would sit down on a curb in front of someone's house or lie down on someone's lawn. As you drove up McCloud Avenue toward Pearls house, you would often see a few of her visitors sprawled on the ground of the vacant lot on the corner.

When Pearl went to the store, older townspeople would occasionally come up to her and say something like, "Well, you're pretty cozy with those dirty hippies. I hear that they come here to see you."

Finally, she had had enough, and called a meeting at her house. She invited the heads of the Chamber of Commerce, Pacific Power and Light Company, the Bank of America, pastors of local churches, real estate brokers, and the Chief of Police. While everyone sipped tea and ate

---

[47] See *Adventures of a Western Mystic, Part I: Apprentice to the Masters* by Peter Mt. Shasta, Chapter 3 (Church of the Seven Rays, 2010).

the cookies she had baked, she said, "I am very concerned about the way these young kids coming to town are being treated. They are good kids, and deserve to be treated better. Weren't you young once? Didn't you ever want to break out of your mold and be free? That is what the kids are doing, and they want to make a better world. All I am asking is that you give them a chance. Open your hearts to them, and make them feel welcome."

Many nodded their heads in agreement, but a few said, "Why don't they cut their hair and wear decent clothes if they want to be accepted?"

"I will see what I can do, but give it some time," Pearl said. "By the way, these kids may look like poor waifs, but some of them are actually quite wealthy."

"That's true; they are buying houses," a couple of real estate agents chimed in.

The next time I saw Pearl, she said in her diplomatic way, "Some people find that when they move to a new town, they are more accepted if their appearance does not set them apart."

As I walked down the hill afterward, I thought, "Was that a hint that I should change my appearance?" I was still wearing the white Indian clothes that were the norm in India, but to westerners looked like pajamas. My hair and beard were also long and scraggly, and although I thought of myself as a wandering yogi, I certainly gave the appearance of being a hippie. "I suppose I could cut my hair," I thought.

A few weeks later when I got into the real estate business, I began to have the urge to join the Chamber of Commerce. I resisted, as that commercial organization seemed to represent everything I had embarked on the spiritual path to avoid, but the urge became stronger and stronger. Finally, I surrendered to the feeling and attended a meeting of the Chamber at a popular diner by the freeway. I sat on one side of the back room, in my baggy clothes and long hair, and the rest of the businessmen in town sat on the other sides, all seeming to wear the polyester "leisure suits" that were then the fashion.

I was surprised when I was introduced as a guest, and further shocked at the end of the meeting, when the managers of the Bank of America and Pacific Power and Light both came up to me and welcomed me with hearty handshakes.

The next day I cut my hair and bought my own leisure suit. At the next meeting, although still feeling inwardly like a yogi, I fit right in with the other businessmen.[48]

When Pearl saw me in my new persona, she smiled and said, "You got it." She confessed that she had talked to the Masters to ask them to inspire us to fit in better in the rural logging community. Gradually I saw my friends also change their appearances, get jobs, and start their own businesses.

---

48  The Tibetan Lama, Trungpa Rinpoche, said that if you want to change society, first you need to be a part of it.

*Lady Master Pearl*

## 26

### *A Near Ascension*

There was a girl in town we called The Butterfly, as she seemed to flit around bringing joy wherever she lit. One day I was sitting at a table in the health food store where I worked part time, when she came in and sat with me. We exchanged a few words, and then she reached over and took hold of my hand, looking deeply into my eyes. Energy flowed from her hand into mine, and I felt the room swimming in Light. I felt that I was dissolving into her phosphorescent blue eyes, which seemed to be getting larger as my connection with the Earth dissolved. I felt the only thing holding me back was the pain where she was holding my hand. Just when I felt I couldn't take it anymore, she let go.

"Hi, I'm Amana," she said nonchalantly.

"You should see Pearl," I said, holding my hand under the table so that she would not hold it again.

"Well, maybe I should, since you're the third person to tell me that."

I gave her Pearl's phone number and did not see her again for a long time.

A week later I saw Pearl and she said, "That girl you sent came to see me."

For some reason she had felt to take Amana into her bedroom at the back of the house—a first, because Pearl kept her personal space private. She had sat on the edge of her bed, Amana in a chair facing her. Pearl had reached out and taken hold of her hands, and she described the same experience I had, except this time Amana actually rose out of the chair and began to float upward.

"You are ascending," Pearl said.

"Oh, am I?" she asked, in total innocence.

"Yes, are you ready to go?" Pearl asked.

"Well, I don't know," she answered, settling back down in her chair.

Once more, Amana turned her attention inward and began to ascend. On the third time, Pearl was sure that she would go all the way and dissolve into Light. But Amana suddenly relaxed with a sigh, and the room returned to normal.

Amana said she would think about what Pearl had said about ascending, and come back and see her when she had her answer. After she left, Jerry came out of the living room where he had gone to read the newspaper, and said, "What was going on in there?"

"What do you mean?"

"I thought the whole house was going up," Jerry said. "I felt that everything was dissolving."

"Yes, I thought so too," Pearl said.

Amana returned a few weeks later, and again they retreated to Pearl's room. This time nothing out of the ordinary happened, and Amana said, "I just met a wonderful man, and think I'm falling in love with him. I've never had a relationship with a spiritual partner before, so I want to stay and see what it's like."

Soon Amana and her partner left town, moving south to a rural area in the hills of the Sierra Nevada Mountains.

Years later I visited them and was surprised to see that this angelic being was now a grounded mother. She had two young children, a boy and a girl, who clutched at her legs as she cooked dinner. When she greeted me with a hug there was none of the amazing energy I had once felt. Years later I heard that she was diagnosed with cancer, and passed on suddenly. It seemed that being a mother was the last earthly experience her soul craved.

*Lady Master Pearl*

## 27

## *Pearl's Advice to Women*

Immersed in meditation one morning, Pearl and I were disturbed by a knock at the door. Gloria, a red headed girl who had moved to town from New Jersey recently, burst into the living room, threw herself into a chair, and sobbed to Pearl, "What have you done to my husband?"[49]

"What do you mean?"

"I want to know what's going on here—what are you doing that my husband finds so irresistible? What do you want with him?"

"I have no interest in your husband," Pearl replied, "I have one of my own."

"Then why is my husband up here at your house every spare minute? I make love to him every way I can think of, but as soon as he can get out of the house, he comes up here to be with you. What is it that you do?" the girl pleaded.

"Maybe he wants *this*," Pearl said, pointing to her heart.

"What?" Gloria responded, her eyes widening.

---

[49] Even though Pearl was in her 60s, wore plain clothes, and was of ordinary appearance, she was without a doubt the most popular woman in town. See *Adventures of a Western Mystic, Part I: Apprentice to the Masters* by Peter Mt. Shasta, (Church of the Seven Rays, 2010), Ch.12.

"The Pure Christ Love," Pearl replied, sending a beam of that pure essence to the girl's heart.

"Give me a break!" the girl exclaimed. "You expect me to believe that? He doesn't believe in Jesus; he's not into religion. You've put some kind of spell on him."

"As I said," Pearl repeated, "what he feels here is the Pure Christ Love, and no amount of romance or sex can replace that. The Christ Light is the energy of the male and female joined together in the heart, the *marriage made in heaven* that depends on no outer condition—the love that is independent of and precedes all outer relationship. Once someone awakens into that love, all human activity becomes secondary. That is why your husband comes here, because he feels that light which nurtures the Christ within him."

Gloria's eyes opened wider, as though she had been hit by a brick. "What!" she exclaimed, speechless. As she began to feel the love Pearl was sending, her anger abated and she leaned forward. "How did you do that? Is that love something I can learn?"

"Turn your attention inward," Pearl said, again pointing to her heart. "Feel in that soft, vulnerable place within you that is the center of your being, the love that is always there. Feel the love of the Divine Presence that has been waiting, waiting, waiting throughout the ages for you to turn your attention to It, wondering how long you will give energy to outer people, places, conditions, and things—waiting for you to give your obedience to It. That is the Christ Light, and that is what your husband is after."

As Gloria began to feel the spark Pearl had kindled in her heart, she relaxed in her chair and her eyes closed. I watched, amazed, as the girl's breathing softened and her face became radiant as an angel. In a minute she opened her eyes, which were filled with tears.

"Now I understand why he's been spending so much time with you," she sighed. This is what I want, too. I want to know how to do what you do."

"It is so simple," Pearl said with sadness. "But, so few want this truth. So few are willing to give up pursuing outer things long enough to calm down, be still, and know *I AM God.*"

Gloria's outburst still fresh in my mind, and curious about the Masters' teaching on relationship, love, and sex, I asked Pearl the next day to tell me more about how these powerful drives affect the spiritual path. Referring to what had happened the day before, Pearl said, "Jealousy is a poison, and it comes from not knowing who you are, of thinking that your Source is in someone else, of not feeling the source of happiness within yourself. That ignorance of the Presence," Pearl continued, "is what leads people mistakenly to think that through relationship they can find what they lack, rather than finding completion within. Once one has found the bliss of union with God, no sex or romance can hold one's attention for long, for the all-consuming romance is with one's *I AM,* the *God Presence.*

"Furthermore, the feeling that one's mate is a possession destroys not only the relationship but also obstructs progress on the spiritual path for both. True love can only take place where there is freedom. Freedom does not mean the liberty to indulge your passions of the moment, but the free dominion that comes from following and being obedient to your own God Source. For both partners to support each other in that quest is the ideal relationship.

"If you only knew how many married people come to me and say, 'Oh, if I could only be single, then I would make such spiritual progress.' And the single ones come and say, 'Oh, if only I had a partner, then I would be happy.'

"You cannot avoid your feelings. You cannot avoid your passions. No matter what you do, they will come to the surface and influence your thoughts, words, and actions. You can be a yogi in a cave for a while, and because you don't see your delusions anymore you think they are gone, but when you return to the world, they will reassert themselves. Better to be in the world and face your miscreated energy with the light of conscious awareness. That is why relationship can be the fast path to self-purification, because your partner is your mirror—to show you where the real work is.

"Sometimes you may be in a relationship, sometimes alone," Pearl continued, "Both are appropriate for different times of one's development. But either way, you need to take responsibility for your feelings. Only you are responsible for your own thoughts, emotions, and actions, not anyone else. So, the source of your happiness and freedom is not in someone else, but in your self. You came into the world alone and you leave the world alone. You can walk with another only part of the way. Make that be a walk into the light, helping each other attain self mastery."

# 28

## *You Are Ready*

My training in Mastery took me into real estate, buying old houses, fixing them up, and renting them out. Eventually I got a real estate license and worked in an office; however, my heart was always with Pearl and the Ascended Masters, and whenever I could get away from showing houses I would go see her. There were always people there, and sometimes she would fall silent and ask me to do the talking.

"What do you want me to talk about, Pearl?" I often asked, and she would reply with a shrug. After a moment of silence, she would say, "Why not turn your attention to your I AM Presence, and see what comes forth?"

I would start my day at 8 am, and before running off to deal with complaining tenants, building contractors, accountants, and attorneys, I would walk two minutes uphill to see Pearl, and we would sit in meditation. After work or after dinner, I would again go to her house and either sit alone with her or participate in whatever group happened to be there. Often she would ask me to talk, but I always tried to remain silent. After all, she was the teacher. I didn't realize at the time that asking me to talk was the teaching. She was trying to prepare me for the work for which the Masters had sent me there.

One day I was shocked when she looked fixedly at me and said, "You're ready."

"Oh, ready for what?" I asked, perplexed.

"Why do you think I have been training you all these years? Saint Germain told me this morning that you are ready to begin working."

"What kind of work?" My mind was a blank.

"Helping people. Isn't that what you want? It's been three years and three months since you first came to see me, since you sat in that chair and asked to be of assistance to Saint Germain. Now it is time for you to get busy."

"But I have no idea what to do," I complained.

She gave me a penetrating look, and after a minute of silence, she said, "You could say,

*I AM the Resurrection and the Life of my
Divine Mission on Earth, now made manifest.*

"I assure you, this work was laid out before your birth. Now it is time to begin, and nothing can forestall that, so get ready. Do you think that I planned to do this work, that I thought I was ready? No, people just started showing up."

I left her house feeling queasy at what might be coming. I had to admit, I knew her teachings inside and out, but the idea of sitting in front of a group was not what I had in mind. I was much more comfortable sitting in silent absorption of the Ascended Master Consciousness that permeated her living room. I was used to the freedom of being able to get up and go whenever I wanted.

However, soon all my rental properties sold and my real estate business seemed to dissolve. In a miraculously short time I was free. As most of the houses were in poor condition and did not qualify for bank financing, I had to finance the sales myself. I took payment in the form of promissory notes that gave me enough residual income to sustain me for many years. As my attorney, Arnie Breyer, said, to paraphrase the Yiddish, "I fell into an outhouse but came out smelling like a rose."

One day, sitting on my sofa, there was a knock at the door. As I opened it, I was surprised to see Isha Kaur, a girl I had met many years before at an ashram in Phoenix, and who had led me into the desert on a journey of initiation.[50] Now she was standing before me with a group of friends.

"It's good to see you again, Peter. May we come in?"

"Yes, of course," I stammered. "What brings you to Mount Shasta?"

"We came to see Pearl, and she said that she was too busy to see us, so she sent us to see you."

"Oh," was all I could say, seized by a moment of panic. "What am I supposed to do?" I wondered, wishing that Pearl were there.

The three of them, Isha, Fred, and Dharma, sat in a semi-circle, waiting for something to happen, but they did not have to wait long. The moment we sat, I called on my I AM Presence and the Ascended Masters to bring about

---

50  Initiation is a term signifying any experience, ritual, or empowerment that leads one inward to a greater sense of one own Divinity. To read about this particular initiation, read my autobiographical book, *Adventures of a Western Mystic, Part II: Search for the Guru* (Church of the Seven Rays, 2013) Ch. 65, "The Goddess of Phoenix."

the Divine Plan, and as they talked I visualized each one's I AM Presence above them. Soon an aura of Divine Energy began to infuse the room.

All fell silent, and entered into an effortless absorption in the Oneness. After a while, when we returned to a more mundane awareness, I was able to answer a few of their questions. As the words flowed effortlessly, I realized now how well Pearl had trained me. It seemed that once more Isha Kaur had been instrumental in an initiation, this time helping to push me into my true service.

A few days after Isha and her group left, a friend they had met in town told me of Fred's experience that afternoon in my living room. He had never believed in God and had always been skeptical of spiritual things. He was especially suspicious of the legends about miraculous things happening around Mount Shasta, but he said to his friend, "If there is a God that exists, I experienced Him that afternoon."

That was the beginning, and throughout the summer the flow of visitors increased. Now I understood what Pearl experienced every day. People showed up at all hours, and I was lucky to grab a handful of fruit or nuts to munch in the interim between visitors; although, in that energy field I hardly needed to eat at all. My gratitude for her training and the sacrifices she had made continually increased. I did not realize it at the time, but she was beginning to shift some of her burden to me in preparation for her own Ascension.

*Peter Mt. Shasta*

*Peter Mt. Shasta, circa 1984.*

## 29

## *An Inner Marriage*

One day as I was walking through Dunsmuir, a small town just south of Mount Shasta, I noticed a small curio shop I had never seen before. Normally, I would have walked past a place like this, as there was nothing about its dingy exterior or the used items in its dirty window that I would have found appealing. However, for some reason that I can only describe as the pull of inner guidance, I found myself entering.

When an elderly woman came out of the back room and asked if she could help, I said no, that I was just looking, but at that moment my eyes fell on a pair of matched rings, each with a gleaming ruby in them. When I asked how much they cost, and she said four dollars each, I knew that they could not possibly be real. Yet, there was something magical about them; and even though I was not one to wear rings, the same force that had led me into the shop caused me to buy the pair—as they seemed to belong together.

Next morning when I saw Pearl, I still had the rings in my pocket, and drew them out to show her. Suddenly, I felt the inexplicable impulse to give her one. Surprisingly, instead of holding out her hand, she extended the ring finger of her left hand. As I slid it over her finger, she then asked for the other ring, which she slid over my finger.

"What just happened?" I wondered. I had a feeling that it was something important, but of what significance?

The feeling that I was missing something increased when Pearl asked, "Don't you remember?"

"Remember what?" I asked.

"Never mind, you will remember when the time is right."

That night as I went to bed, I asked, "Saint Germain, please show me everything I need to know about this ring," then fell asleep. Soon I was in the retreat at the Royal Teton, in Saint Germain's private audience chamber. Pearl and I were there, wearing exquisite gowns, and Saint Germain was standing before us. He took our hands in his and said, "Peter and Pearl, my beloved students, I join you together once more in spiritual union. This is a soul connection that has been in existence for millennia. I am now renewing your association for the work you have to do together now."

Then he joined our hands together and bound them with a golden cord. The next thing I knew it was morning. I rose and looked at the ruby ring sitting on the night table, and realized now why Pearl had regarded the gift of the ring as so important.

## 30

### *Pearl and Jerry*

Jerry was always a mysterious, silent man in the background, an enigma to many. One day, after I had been meditating with Pearl and felt raised above the Earth, she said, "Why don't you go out back and talk to Jerry?"

I knew this was a request, so I went out the back door to the garage. There he was, standing in front of a worktable full of tools, which were all in their proper places, pounding something on an anvil.

"Hi, Jerry, what are you up to?"

"Straightening nails."

"Oh, really?"

"No point in wasting them. They're still perfectly good."

"I suppose so."

I continued to watch for several minutes, wondering what Pearl had intended me to learn, then said goodbye. Another time, Pearl also suggested that I "talk with Jerry," who was in front of the house, working on the gate in the hedge at the beginning of the path leading to the front door.

"Hi, Jerry, fixing the gate?"

"Yup, it was beginning to squeak, but it just needed a few drops of oil."

"Nice day, isn't it?"

"Sure is."

Again, I left wondering what teaching I was to derive from this encounter. Only later did I begin to see him as a Zen master. Although conscious on many levels, he was able to focus almost totally on the work of the present moment.

"Well, did you learn anything from Jerry?" Pearl asked the day after one of these visits.

"He seems very peaceful," was all I could think of saying.

"Yes, he is, but the cows are peaceful too." Then she continued, "Sometimes that peace drives me crazy and I want a little excitement. I ran away from him a couple of times, but each time he came and brought me home." Her confession shocked me, for I had always seen them as an idyllic couple, never dreaming that she had ever felt discontent—as she presented the image of the happy wife.

"One day I'd had enough, and ran away to Portland. I wasn't there a week when I had a dream. I was falling out of a tower and Jerry caught me. So I realized that he was sent for my support and protection. The next day Jerry found me and said, 'Time to come home, Pearl.'

"'Yes, I know,' I said, and got in the car.

"After we arrived home Saint Germain appeared and said, 'Pearl, there is no stopping a filly, but first she needs to be broken,' implying that I was the filly. You see, Jerry used to break horses, so I saw that the Master had brought Jerry into my life to discipline my willfulness. Without him, I would be on the Mountain living the carefree life like the rest of you."

In many people's eyes Jerry was a saint. He worked full

time downtown, and when he came home at noon Pearl was usually too busy seeing people to make him anything to eat. In the evening it was often the same, although she did make an effort to keep an hour clear for them to have dinner alone. Even then, they were frequently interrupted by the ring of the phone or a knock at the door.

One evening when Pearl's work first started, there was a knock at the door after dinner. Pearl and Jerry were sitting in the living room, Pearl crocheting and Jerry reading the paper. "Tell them to come back tomorrow," Jerry said, "We have the right to at least some privacy."

Pearl greeted the young man who stood in the doorway, backpack in hand, and said, "I can't see you tonight. Come back tomorrow."

"Oh," the young man said, crestfallen, as he picked up his pack and walked out through the gate and down the street.

As Pearl started back to the living room, Saint Germain appeared and said, "Pearl, I sent that boy to you because he needed help. Don't ever disobey me again."

She ran back to the door to call the man back, but he was gone. Returning to the living room, she told Jerry what had happened, that she was working for the Masters, and she needed his cooperation.

"Very well, I believe you, Pearl," Jerry said. "I will do whatever I can to help you."

From then on, whenever Jerry was home, he answered the phone, made appointments, and greeted visitors at the door. He would often accompany guests into the living room and sit down with them for a while, listening to Pearl teach as though he were experiencing her for the first time.

Gone were his evenings in the easy chair with his paper and the TV. Many evenings he sat alone in his bedroom, ready to answer the phone so its ringing would not interrupt Pearl's work. Only eighteen years later, after they moved to Yreka, did he regain his privacy—giving him time to do his own spiritual work in preparation for his Ascension.

I had never thought of Jerry as much more than Pearl's supporter and protector, until one day when I was in Los Angeles, sleeping on a friend's floor, and I woke in the middle of the night to find Jerry kneeling beside me. Although he was in his etheric body, he appeared just as real as back home. After explaining what I needed to do in the present situation, he said that he would give me his protection, and then disappeared. I realized then that he was far more advanced than I had known.

Years later, when I visited Pearl and Jerry in Yreka, I felt that Pearl had become more a friend, while Jerry had become my teacher. Seeing how he lived a contemplative life in service to Pearl, I understood the selfless compassion of a Master.

# 31

## *Step By Step We Climb*

After she had finished editing the last volume of *Life and Teachings of the Masters of the Far East,* Pearl's friend, Sunny Widell had gone in search of other spiritual teachers to whom she could offer her service as an executive secretary or literary editor. First she worked for Geraldine Innocente, another former student of Godfre Ray King, who in 1951 started the Bridge to Freedom organization to further spread the Masters' teachings. However, Sunny did not feel the Masters' spiritual radiation as she had when Godfre talked, so she moved on. She then went to work for Mark and Elizabeth Prophet, also former students of the Saint Germain Foundation. However, when she saw how extensively Elizabeth rewrote the "dictations of the Masters," she resigned. Finally, Sunny moved to Mount Shasta to live a quiet life in the aura of the Mountain.

She frequently offered her services to Pearl, toward whom she felt great admiration and loyalty, which sometimes took the form of cleaning the house. One morning in the spring of 1976, Sunny was helping Pearl clean the attic, when she discovered a carton filled with manuscripts. They turned out to be the discourses from the Masters through Pearl and Bob to the group of former I AM students that had gathered in the period from 1940–1945. Overjoyed at her discovery, she said, "Pearly, these discourses are a treasure. They need to be published so that everyone can read them."

Pearl consented, and let Sunny take the box home to peruse the discourses as she wished, and to put them in a suitable format for publication. However, knowing that Sunny was out of touch with the New Age trend, she requested that Sunny allow a small group of her closest students to assist. The discourses contained personal messages that pertained only to matters pertinent at that time, as well as much that was repetitive, and that extraneous material needed to be deleted for clearer reading. A few of Pearl's trusted students and I participated in this process. However, Sunny, who had never understood the hippie phenomenon, and who now resented them taking so much of Pearl's time, began complaining more and more adamantly to Pearl about their "interference" with her project. As with any editorial project, there were differences of opinion, but Pearl did not set up any structure for resolving these differences, and the fiery-tempered Sunny did not understand the principle of compromise. In desperation at being besieged with complaints by Sunny on one hand and by her students on the other, she recalled the manuscript that she had named *Step By Step We Climb*.

One morning as I sat with Pearl, she placed a large object wrapped in plain brown paper in my lap and said, "I turn this over to you."

"What is it?"

"It's the manuscript. You can do what you want with it; publish it or throw it in the trash, just so long as I never have to hear about it again."

"Really?" I asked, overwhelmed at suddenly being given a collection of discourses from the Masters.

"Yes, and I never want to hear another thing about it," she emphasized.

At the time, neither of us realized the series of events that this transfer would set in motion. As I knew Pearl did not act without consulting her I AM Presence and Saint Germain, I assumed that everything about the book's publication would now flow smoothly. I did not realize that sometimes the Masters shake things up for some higher purpose that the people involved cannot see. This shakeup now began.

Pearl had neglected to tell Sunny and the rest of our Pearl Publishing editorial group (Steve Bollock, Gene and Mary Duda, Bill Gaum, Leila Whitcomb, and others) that she had given the manuscript to me as my sole responsibility, so I flew off to the East Coast to find a publisher, blissfully unaware of the catastrophe that was about to take place. I finished the editing, which at this point consisted mostly of correcting punctuation and formatting, and flew down to Georgia to meet with CSA Press in Lakemont. I thought it auspicious when they told me it was situated on an amethyst mine.

However, that auspiciousness did not protect me from what then took place, and which effectively damaged my relationship with Pearl for the next couple of years. Hearing that the book was about to be published without her input, Sunny contacted the printer and told them that I had stolen the manuscript. Threatened by a lawsuit, they returned it to me. Despite my pleas to Pearl to straighten things out, she did not tell Sunny or any of our group that she had given me complete authority. Nor did Pearl contact the printer and correct the accusation. As I was one of Pearl's star pupils, with many close friends in the group (including Steve Bollock, on whom Pearl relied heavily) the dissention that followed created chaos—and over the next year Pearl's group began to dissolve. Years later, I began to write my autobiography, *Adventures of a Western Mystic,* and Steve rented me a room in his home in the woods next to the Saint Germain Amphitheater.

It was the Masters' way of dissolving a structure that had performed its usefulness, and of empowering each individual to go out and apply the teachings they had learned sitting at her feet. It also freed Pearl to leave Mount Shasta, a move that would leave her time to prepare for her Ascension.

*Step by Step We Climb* would finally be published in 1977 by a small press in Happy Camp, in the hills west of Yreka. *"I AM" the Open Door,* the small book of discourses the Masters gave me, would be published the same year. Ironically, the painful separation that Pearl had gone through with Mrs. Ballard had now gone full circle. Just as Mrs. Ballard had rejected her book, *"I AM" America's Destiny,* Pearl now rejected the book the Masters had given me.

Torn by this conflict, Pearl came down with a painful case of shingles, and I suffered from the rumors that spread through town. To get out of this vortex, I moved in with friends, ten miles north in Weed, ironically on Division Street. Sunny passed on a couple of years later, never having understood that the Masters had set up this conflict to bring about growth. The healing between Pearl and me would come a few years later through the spiritual insight of a young man named Bill Gaum, who would assist Pearl and Jerry to make their transitions.

One day in 1982, Pearl and Jerry were on one of their long drives through the country around Mount Shasta. She said that often they channeled Light into the earth, or invoked it for the people who lived in the towns through which they passed. On their return home they decided to stop in Yreka, forty miles to the north, and as they pulled into town Pearl heard the voice of her I AM Presence say, "A two-bedroom house, buy, don't rent." She had never liked Yreka, an old mining town built over abandoned mine shafts. However, she knew better than to argue with her Higher Self, so she told Jerry what she had heard, and they bought a newspaper to see what was available.

Jerry spotted an entry in the real estate section that sounded interesting, so they phoned the seller. It turned out to belong to the owners of Nature's Kitchen, a health food store and restaurant that was one of the bright spots in town. They looked at the house, and both got the feeling to go ahead. Back at Nature's Kitchen, as they were talking with the owner, Pearl heard, "Write the check now." She told Jerry, who by now had come to trust Pearl's intuition, and he wrote out the check and handed it to the owner. Just as they shook hands on the deal, a man walked in and announced, "I finally decided to buy your house, and here's my check." But the owners told him he was too late.

Pearl and Jerry moved into the house in a quiet neighborhood on South West Street. Some students still made the occasional pilgrimage to visit her, but she had an increasing amount of time to do her inner work. Now that Jerry had retired, he too had more time on his hands, and he went for walks around the town. However, he missed the activity of Mount Shasta.

Without having to give so much of her time and energy to the dozens of people who came to see her every day, Pearl was now able to work on her own ascension process. Many who held her hands reported that she seemed increasingly etheric—as though they were hardly touching anyone. With this increase in vibratory rate, she found that her sustenance came directly from the Source, and she no longer needed to eat. Gradually she no longer needed to converse with her I AM Presence to receive guidance, for as duality ended she began to merge with It in consciousness.

Two years later they suddenly moved to Fort Jones, in the valley west of Yreka. It was guidance that took Pearl and Jerry by surprise, as they were comfortably settled in Yreka, but they completed the move anyway, without the Masters having provided any explanation. During that time Bill Gaum, who had met Pearl previously, returned for a visit. He had recently graduated with a Masters degree in Public Administration, with a specialization in foreign policy, and had just returned from interning with a U. S. Congressman in Washington, DC. Before he looked for a job in government, he wanted to consult with Pearl, and through her, the Ascended Masters. To his great surprise, the guidance came to him directly, that instead of applying for a job in government, he should offer his assistance to Pearl and Jerry. They were now almost eighty, and needed an increasing amount of help. He thought it was going to be a temporary assignment, but it turned out to be a service that would occupy him for the next six years.

As Bill found himself spending more and more time with them, almost like a son, Jerry offered him a place to stay in the camper they had parked in front of the garage. When they went to move it one day so they could open the door, they discovered the battery was dead, and the engine wouldn't crank over. Even the lights would not work.

As Bill and Jerry sat in the cab trying to figure out what to do, Pearl came out and asked, "What's the problem, boys?"

"The battery's dead," Jerry said.

"Well, you just stay there and I'll see what I can do," Pearl said.

Jerry shrugged, as if to say there was no harm in trying, and he and Bill watched as Pearl stood at the front of the car and put both hands on the hood. After a moment of silence, she said, "OK, try it now."

As soon as Jerry turned the ignition key, the engine roared to life. Jerry turned to Bill and with his wry sense of humor said, "Pearl's still got quite a bit of power."

After pulling the truck forward, Bill was now able to access his new bedroom inside. It wasn't a plush condo in Washington, or the job at the center of governmental power for which he'd gone to school for so many years, but it was definitely employment on behalf of the Great White Brotherhood.[51]

---

51 The Great White Brotherhood, despite its name, contains women, as well as different races. It has also been called the Great Lodge or the Hierarchy.

*Lady Master Pearl*

During their stay in Fort Jones, which in 1851 had been the site of the massacre of the Shasta Tribe, Pearl realized that she had been sent there to help assist those souls from that tribe who were still earthbound to attain their freedom. There were also beings from a previous age trapped there in the astral realm, whom she worked on liberating. She would sit up in bed, talking to these spirits who some would call ghosts, hearing of their sorrows, and guiding them to the Light. She would call on the Angels of the Violet Flame and Archangel Michael to dissolve whatever remaining karma they had, and raise them to a higher dimension where they could continue their evolution. After about a month in Fort Jones, Pearl realized that her work there was done, and that it was time to go home. Bill helped them pack, and soon they were back in Yreka.

Visitors occasionally came from Mount Shasta or drove down from Oregon to see Pearl, although the number was much reduced. Many of Pearl's previous students continued to drop in, but there were also a few new students who had heard of Pearl's connection with the Masters, and how people's lives had been changed in her presence. Many simply came to be near her, and to feel the love she emanated.

One day a couple of ladies who were professional psychics arrived, and when Pearl asked why they had come, they said, "Since we have been channeling you for years, we finally wanted to come see you."

Pearl and Bill thought this was humorous, as Pearl had taught for years that channeling was usually the product of an undisciplined ego coupled with overactive imagination, if not possession by a discarnate entity (earthbound soul). She said the Masters stressed that, even if you could channel a Master, channeling does not lead to Mastery. That can only be achieved by overcoming the lower self, through disciplining the mind and ego.

One day in 1986, Pearl began to feel an acceleration of her vibratory rate, a raising process during which she felt she was leaving the Earth. Receiving a phone call that her Twin Ray, Bob, had passed on in his sleep, she realized that, because of their unity, she was participating in his Ascension. This process lasted three days, but after that Pearl was not the same. She was even more etheric, and no longer needed to eat or sleep.

Soon, Pearl received a second shock when Jerry had a heart attack. Sitting with him in the Yreka Hospital, she held his hand, knowing he was making the transition. Just before he passed on, he looked into her eyes and said, "You are so beautiful." He repeated it again with great wonder in his eyes, and then left his body.

Pearl said that Jerry had healed her through his patience, and had made her own spiritual evolution possible. His strength, tempered with gentleness, had helped her achieve completion in this life.

*Lady Master Pearl*

*Jerry Dorris at home in Mt. Shasta, circa 1975.*

## 32

## *Bill's Revelation*

One evening after Pearl went to bed, Bill felt the pull to pick up the copy of *"I AM" the Open Door*, the book of discourses the Masters had transmitted to me in their visible light bodies in 1977. As Bill began reading the first lines by the Great Divine Director, he felt the radiation of the Masters coursing through him. In the morning when he told Pearl what he had felt, and that he thought the discourses were authentic, Pearl admitted that she had never read the book. When Bill then placed it in her hands, the veil was lifted in the drama whose purpose was known only to the Ascended Masters. She, too, then felt the energy that only ones that are Ascended can give, and said, crestfallen, "Oh, I have made a terrible mistake. I need to apologize to Peter."

While in my second-floor office in Mount Shasta, I heard the sound of two people ascending the creaking stairs.[52] To my great surprise, there was Pearl, standing before me, with Bill beside her. After they sat down, Bill said, "Pearl asked me to bring her here, as she would like to do something for you."

Pearl said, "I realize that I have committed a wrong,

---

[52] I was given an office by Dr. William S. Leonard at Pendragon Clinic, 630 N. Mt. Shasta Blvd., Mount Shasta, where I practiced astrology and natural healing.

and to make up for that I would like to publish, *"I AM" the Open Door* as a paperback if you would like. It carries the energy of the Masters, and I want to make it more available to people."

While I was still astounded by her offer, she leaned forward and took my hands in hers, and looked into my eyes as she had in the past. In those seconds, the ancient bond was renewed, and we recognized the eternal love that required no words. After that timeless moment she rose, and with Bill holding her hand they descended the stairs.

A few weeks later we drove to visit the printer in Happy Camp to arrange publication, and in a few months the paperback was in our hands. It soon became a metaphysical bestseller (now translated into German and French and available as an audiobook from Audible.com), and in those last few years of her life, Pearl frequently gave it to many who came to see her.

## 33

### *Pearl's Ascension*

During the last few years I had become closer to Pearl even than before our separation, perhaps because I was no longer her student, but now a friend. Frequently, she, Bill, and I would go out to lunch together in Mount Shasta. These meetings were arranged completely on the inner planes. There were no cell phones, texts, or emails in those days, and I would simply see Pearl's face before me and feel the pull to go outside. Bill would just then be pulling up at the curb, or I would be walking down the street and their car would pull up alongside. We frequently went to Lalo's Mexican Restaurant and asked for a single plate of *huevos rancheros* with three plates. Bill would eat the beans and rice, and I ate the eggs and tortillas. When confronted by Bill that she should eat something, Pearl would put a leaf of lettuce on her plate, and nibble a few bites. The waitress came to the table once, and seeing that Pearl hadn't eaten anything, asked with concern, "Wouldn't you like more to eat?"

"No, thank you, I haven't eaten in two years," Pearl replied.

"But, aren't you hungry?" the waitress asked in shock. "How do you live?"

"I live on love," Pearl replied with a smile.

Much shaken, the waitress departed.

The Masters offered Pearl her Ascension three times during the last few years of her life. One time she was before a group in her home, and another time following a stroke two days after Christmas, in 1987. Each time she said, "I will stay in this body as long as there is anyone I can help." However, the Masters finally told her to make preparations, that she could no longer delay, and on August 9th, 1990 she announced to Bill, "I am beginning the Ascension, and the Great Ones are helping me."[53] She described a ceremony taking place in a higher dimension, in which she was being welcomed into the realm of the Ascended Masters. That raising process continued on into October as she gradually became more and more conscious in her Higher Mental Body. A week prior to her passing, a group sitting by her bed heard beautiful music and became enveloped in a circle of light. This raising process finally completed early on the morning of October 19th, 1990, when, during her sleep, she severed the last tie to her physical body.

Bill said that the house seemed bathed in Light. As she had requested, there was no funeral, but her body was held for three days, and then cremated. A group of her former students gathered in her home on October 21st, the day after what would have been her 85th birthday, to express their gratitude. Bill said that it was the most powerful group meditation he had ever experienced.

---

53 The details of Pearl's ascension are from *The Life and Teachings of Pearl Dorris, an American Saint*, by Bill Gaum (unpublished manuscript, copyright by Gill Gaum, 2001). For more information, and to read excerpts from Pearl's books, see his website: www.manypathsleadtogod.com.

I had visited Pearl in August, but at the time of her passing was in Arizona, where my daughter had just been born. I had always assumed that when she left her body there would be rainbows in the sky, as frequently happens on the passing of Tibetan Lamas. Or, I would dream of the Masters escorting her to a higher plane amid choirs of angels, but to my great disappointment I experienced nothing. I had to rely on Bill's account of her Ascension process, and had no inner contact with Pearl for over a year. Then, gradually she began to visit in dreams. She indicated that she was free, and no longer needed to return in a physical form.

Then in 2012, two years after my autobiography, *Adventures of a Western Mystic: Apprentice to the Masters,* was published, she began to come more tangibly. As the book aroused interest among spiritual seekers, I began to receive invitations to give talks to various groups. One of these talks took place in Los Angeles across the street from Universal Studios. A woman began interrupting, contradicting me, and trying to take over the group. Suddenly I felt Pearl's presence beside me, and was shocked when she told me to assert myself, as I had seen her do quite strongly on occasion.

As we left we drove past Universal Studios where, in her twenties, Pearl had briefly been an actress in silent films, and I heard her say, "Now you understand what I had to deal with all those years. It is in working with the human ego—that always thinks it knows best—that you face your greatest challenges, as well as achieve your greatest growth."

Although she has not materialized in front of me in physical form the way other Masters have, I am frequently aware of her presence. I feel her especially in my heart, where she resides as a Pearl of Great Price.

> *Again, the kingdom of heaven is like a merchant seeking beautiful pearls who, when he had found one pearl of great price, went and sold all that he had and bought It.*
>
> -Matthew 13:45

Note: Pearl has appeared to many readers of this book, and given a blessing or other personal encouragement. I feel that the appearance of this book at this time marks a turning point in her work, that after the 24 years since her transition into the Ascended State, she is now drawing closer to help those who are students of Saint Germain. She seems especially concerned with helping those in feminine embodiment. You may call to her for assistance by turning your attention inward, saying, and feeling, "I AM the Presence of Pearl."

## *Postscript: A Note on Historical Accuracy*

In the course of the seventeen years I knew Pearl, I heard many of her stories easily fifty times. Yet, she didn't always tell them the same way, and toward the end of her life some of the outer details changed considerably, leaving me in doubt as to when and where certain events had occurred.

A more lengthy biography is being written by Bill Gaum, the man who took care of Pearl and Jerry during their last years, and who has access to her personal records. Bill has allowed me access to this work in progress, and I have cited it as a reference in a number of places; however, my account may have inaccuracies with regard to certain particulars.

An example of how Pearl's accounts often changed over the years was her story of being reprimanded when she told people to say "I AM good." This was a story she told often, explaining how "they" told her, "You can't say that." At first she said that this happened at school, so I assumed "they" were her high school teachers, but later she said "at the college," so I thought "they" were the deans of the business college in Los Angeles. Years later, when she said "in the class," I finally realized "they" were the other staff members of the Saint Germain Foundation, who reprimanded her during a class she taught in San Francisco.

Regardless of the outer change of venue, the core of the experience remained the same; so, rather than not mention an event because I wasn't sure of the exact particulars, I have written what I could to capture the essence of the life of an extraordinary woman—someone who changed the lives of many people and altered how esoteric teachings are given in the West. She never promoted herself, but did not turn away those who found her. She was Everywoman, an ordinary person who could have been your grandmother; yet, as she was empowered by the Christ Light Within, she blessed all whom she met, simply by the power of her love.

*In the West the true teachers are almost completely unknown. Even if you found one of them, you would have to pry out of them what they know.*

-Sathya Sai Baba

## *Read Other Books by Peter Mt. Shasta*

*"I AM" the Open Door,* Discourses by the Ascended Masters, Smashwords edition, audio on iBooks and Audible.com read by Peter Mt. Shasta, and paperback.

*"I AM" Affirmations and the Secret of their Effective Use,* also available in French and German on Smashwords.com, in paperback, and as an audio book read by the author on Audible.com and iBooks.

*Adventures of a Western Mystic, Part I: Search for the Guru,* also available as an eBook and paperback, and in a German paperback edition from www.BoD.de.

*Adventures of a Western Mystic, Part II: Apprentice to the Masters,* available as an eBook, paperback, and in a German paperback edition from www.BoD.de.

To connect with me, please visit my website and blog at ***www.petermtshasta.com.***

*Peter Mt. Shasta at Hakone Gardens, Saratoga, California, 2014. (Photo by Runa Gupta)*

www.ingramcontent.com/pod-product-compliance
Lightning Source LLC
Chambersburg PA
CBHW021126300426
44113CB00006B/310